SAINT THOMAS AQUINAS

SELECTED WRITINGS

SELECTIONS FROM HIS WORKS MADE BY

GEORGE N. SHUSTER

WOOD ENGRAVINGS BY

REYNOLDS STONE

THE HERITAGE PRESS
NEW YORK

Passages from *Philosophical Texts* and *Theological Texts*,
translated by Thomas Gilby, have been used by
arrangement with the Oxford University Press

INTRODUCTION

This book, so beautifully decorated by the engravings of Reynolds Stone, is designed to provide some insight into the thought, wisdom, and personality of the most eminent of medieval scholars, whose influence on philosophical and theological speculation remains powerful in our time. His treatises surpass in volume and scope of concern those of any other seminal thinker, even Hegel, but for the most part they are records of classroom lectures and discussions. Some of them are based on what was said during systematic university courses. But like many another professor, Thomas was willing to meet students and talk about whatever questions seemed of special interest to them. The records of some of these have also been preserved.

Doing all this required an almost incredible amount of preparation. The art of printing had not yet been developed in Europe. The manuscripts, prepared for the most part in monastic writing rooms (*scriptoria*), were often hard to decipher by the light of the sun or of candles. Even so the number of texts available for those who had access to them was large, and the array of authors imposing. Scholars of the medieval period also continued the classical tradition of encyclopedia making and tried to supply convenient compendia of what they thought particularly important. Thomas appears to have read almost everything that seemed significant or interesting to the universities of his time. Much of this was quite new, deriving as it did from Arabian and Jewish sources; and he relied on one of his colleagues in particular for translations. Yet even the mastery of the Christian literature of importance–the Bible, the Church Fathers, Augustine in particular, and the various commentators of the medieval period–would have sufficed to provide reading for a lifetime, which in Thomas's case was relatively brief. Nevertheless, again like scholarly men of our day, he undertook missions for what was then the most illustrious of governments, the Papacy. Astonishingly enough he was also a poet of great distinction. Until the recent changes in the

Liturgy of the Roman Catholic Church, he was probably the most constantly re-read of all writers of religious verse.

The present introduction has been written not by a student of the Thomistic philosophy but by an historian, who was also assigned the task of providing representative texts to illustrate the character of Thomas's thought. An effort was made to assemble texts chosen by contemporary philosophers specially concerned with medieval philosophy, but the attempt was only partly successful. Some of those responding said it was very difficult to answer such a question . . . and not a few of them never did. Others responded discerningly and their suggestions have been followed. Then the editor examined anthologies of Thomistic texts published in several languages and came to the conclusion that the two volumes prepared by Thomas Gilby, O.P., entitled *Philosophical Texts* and *Theological Texts*, best suited his purpose. Two selections are not quoted from his anthologies but from the English version of the *Summa Theologiae*, in the translating and editing of which he had so notable a part. 'The Corpus Christi Sequence' has been adapted by the editor from a traditional version.

It was, to be sure, impossible to reproduce them in their entirety. The selections used in the following pages thus comprise an anthology distilled mostly from anthologies, and arranged according to the editor's own scheme. Briefer quotations are grouped under the general heading of Maxims, while longer selections appear under subject headings. If some readers familiar with Thomas regret not finding passages of special interest to them, others, we shall hope, will gain at least some insight into the life work of one of the most eminent of philosophers and theologians.

The family and social environment into which Thomas Aquinas (Thomas d'Aquino) was born in 1225 was that of the landed gentry of medieval Europe. Their castles, designed as fortresses, were generally primitive in terms of comfort. Their households were bound together by feudal troth to the master. He in turn had a twofold obligation. He was pledged to maintain order in his neighborhood by preventing brigandage and extortion, and to lend assistance to his liege lord in time of war. On the other hand he sought to promote the aggrandizement of his family, not for selfish reasons merely but also because leadership had to be developed and maintained for the benefit of society. His outlook was of course military as his era understood that term, and often enough he proved his valor during the Crusades. Still there was no reason why he should not seek for his children positions of honor and burdensome obligation in Church and State. It is said that Thomas's father, whose castle was Roccasecca, lying along the road from Sicily to Rome, dreamed of his son's becoming Archbishop of Milan.

Instead, having completed preparatory studies in the Benedictine Abbey school of Monte Cassino and having been enrolled in the University of Naples at the age of fifteen, the boy elected to join the then recently founded Dominican Order when he was approximately twenty-seven. This was pledged to defend the integrity and purity of the Christian faith as professed by the Catholic Church, while its sister Mendicant Order, established by St. Francis of Assisi, was more concerned with devotion and works of charity and mercy. Rivalry between them was not unknown, and neither was without its foes within the medieval university. For example, tension at Oxford between the two Orders concerning which was to place its members first in academic processions was resolved by according priority to the Franciscans because of their greater humility! But it proved difficult to persuade University faculties to welcome Mendicants to their midst. For were they not really *vagantes*, tramps, who wandered from place to place, not having what in modern terms is called tenure?

At any rate, north of the Alps Thomas went, probably first of all to Paris and then certainly to Cologne, where he became the disciple of the most illustrious Dominican scholar of the time, the Suabian Albert, later on called Albertus Magnus (Albert the Great). A man of genuinely universal outlook, his constructive criticism of higher education in his time was guided by the maxim that those who had ability and desire to learn should be encouraged to pursue truth no matter where it might be found. It seemed to him inevitable that Aristotelian texts should and would be studied, that nevertheless there was probably something of great value in the speculative method of the Neoplatonists, and that the Natural Sciences must be fostered. No other master could have so greatly influenced the intellectual formation of Thomas. Inevitably, to be sure, the state of learning in his time was a handicap Albert could not surmount and which in turn hampered the most distinguished of his disciples. Both had more insight into the character of scientific method than was until quite recently attributed to them, but they credited Aristotle, their master, with a status as a natural scientist which he did not deserve. Meticulous and imaginative historical scholarship was then also in its infancy, so that they were unable to project adequately the genesis and development of ideas.

But though every modern student of medieval genius is aware of these limitations, the marvel is the ability of Albert and Thomas to emerge nevertheless as seminal thinkers. One major reason is that so many men of distinction had previously served the cause of Christian speculation in philosophy and theology. Stress will be placed here not on the Neoplatonists and the Greek Church Fathers, important though they were, but on three Western thinkers, Boethius, Augustine, and Anselm.

The first, a Roman scholar born during the fifth century, was the author of the *Consolation of Philosophy*, written in prison, and a number of treatises on logic, notably that of Aristotle and Porphyry. The study of logic remained for medieval man something akin to what is today called semantics. Augustine, whose *City of God* was written under the shadow of the fall of the Roman Empire, was by far the greatest thinker of the early Christian centuries. His work reflects the influence of Plato and the Neoplatonists, as well as of Cicero; and probably as a result Platonism was for so long a time a marked part of the medieval synthesis.

Anselm was the first to use the specifically Scholastic method of exposition – that is, statement of a problem, exposition of extant conflicting views concerning it, and the master's own resolution of the problem. Like Thomas, he was born in a castle, the site being Aosta, at the junction of routes leading to the Alpine passes. Destined by his father for a political career, he entered the Benedictine Order instead and eventually became Archbishop of Canterbury. His was a precise and creative mind, concerned on the one hand with the processes of logic in the discovery of reality, and on the other with the concept of Being, which, he urged, found its fullness in God.

Thomas Aquinas proposed a sharp break with this tradition. He accepted the philosophy of Aristotle as the most adequate exposition of cosmic Reality and of man's relationship with it in terms of knowledge and guidance. This he would, however, seek to 'reconcile' with Christian teaching. He would attempt to demonstrate that interpretations of Aristotelian metaphysics, notably those advanced by Arabic philosophers and in some instances accepted in whole or in part by teachers in Christian universities, were false or at least inconclusive. But he would not be, could not be, a literalist in his interpretations of the Aristotelian texts. He would look for guidance to whatever thinker seemed to offer a clue or at least a worthwhile comment. The background for these decisions was supplied by the twelfth century which sundered Anselm from Thomas.

It was a time of dissent, dissatisfaction, and deviation from orthodoxy. Singularly 'open' to all trends in philosophical and theological discussion, it was also 'experimental' in so far as the emotions were concerned. It became evident that the Church which had been so triumphantly institutionalized in the days of Constantine through its association with the State, did not as a matter of fact rule the hearts and minds of men. Influences from the East – on the one hand sectarian in character, and on the other Arabic in the sense that Islamic scholars interpreted the texts of Aristotle in a manner not consonant with Christian orthodoxy – were powerful and persuasive. France was the point of focus, but the impact was felt throughout Europe.

The Crusaders had learned much through their association with the East. That the Holy Spirit was active elsewhere than in the West, that the human conscience must always be respected, that the bad example so often set by Papal Rome must not be permitted to infect the clean of heart, that the brusque monastic way of seeing only carnality in woman was sorely prejudiced – these were some of the notes sounded during this time of incessant change. To be sure, there was genuine reason to believe that the great culture of the ancients, so widely destroyed as a consequence of the fall of Rome, had been restored in broad outline. But there was also widespread poverty; and though two hundred years would pass before Europe would be decimated by the plague known as the Black Death, life expectancy was not high. Royal courts manifested an affluence not previously known in the West, and were often quite worldly in character. At some of the universities the autonomy of human reason was proclaimed while the assumptions of Christian teaching were subjected to remorseless scrutiny.

In the French Provence the Art of Courtly Love was fostered by Queen Eleanor of Aquitaine, and the lyrics of the Troubadours proclaimed the cult of woman. German *Minnesänger* took up the strain. But Provence also witnessed the growth of Eastern sects that preached the contempt for life and love which had been the central concern of the Manicheans against whom Augustine had written one of the most combative of his treatises. The Cathari were the largest of such sects; and against them, once that unaided preaching had failed, the rigors of the Inquisition were invoked. But the full impact of suppressive persecution would not be felt until the next century. Jews too had been widely admitted to cultivated society and their principal writers were read with respect. Such pogroms as had taken place were attributable to outbursts of superstitious wrath on the part of the rabble.

The philosophers meanwhile had become more 'pluralistic' in tone and temper. Perhaps the most gifted among them, Peter Abelard, who evoked the wrath of Bernard of Clairvaux and succumbed to the charms of Eloise, was a perceptive, sensitive thinker, discontented with frozen formulas and a prophet of what would later on be meant by an 'open' society. But Arabic and Jewish speculation generated by far the majority of the controversies. Latin translations of some Aristotelian texts had been available for centuries, but the Arabic commentators, notably Avicenna and Averroes, knew more of them and presented the great Greek in a light incompatible with the Latin tradition. For them he was no 'pious and reverent spirit' but a humanist, a skeptic, and a disbeliever in such fundamental doctrines as the individuality of the human spirit and immortality. Therefore the Christian teacher had either to consign the Arabic philosophers to Limbo or take up the cudgels against them.

Against this turbulent background – made more so by the fact that no one had undertaken the rigorous textual criticism which was obviously required – Thomas took his position as a teacher. Of course he was not immediately what he later became. At first, like every other brilliant young inquirer, he combined groping with flashes of insight. But by the time his great *Summas* were written – one being an exposition of the whole of Theology and the other a critical analysis of the arguments to be employed against the Gentiles – he had created the impressive formulations of the thirteenth century, which though not everywhere accepted were to provide until quite recently the bases for most of Catholic Christian expositions of doctrine.

This remained true also even in the university life of Protestant England during the eighteenth century. Thomas was, to be sure, a critic of the social organization of his time only in the sense that he would have it modified by infusions of charity. He could be critical of authority as exercised by rulers about him, but not of authority as such. Thus he counseled the chieftains to refrain from any war that was not 'just'; but that he ever would have supposed that individuals who had plighted their troth to a liege lord would decide for themselves whether a given war was just or not is quite inconceivable.

What, then, was his conception of philosophical and theological method? It was Aristotelian in philosophy, of course, but never slavishly so. Thomas was determined to look at things as they really are, to the extent that it is possible for a human being to do so. He held that any aspect of the world in which we live can be understood only when all the facts about it have been considered. This was *his* scientific method; and so, in the framework of his time, as has been indicated, he placed great store also by what Aristotle had accomplished as an observer and student of Nature. The Stagirite had of course not anticipated Pasteur, had devised no quantum theory, had known next to nothing about modern genetics. But he had brought the thinking of his epoch into harmony with what was then known. For him as for Thomas, body and soul, sense and intellect, are intimately interwoven. Man reasons best when he proceeds from sense experience to abstraction, and not the other way round.

But that Aristotle's medieval expounder was creative, perceptive, and original has long since been recognized. It becomes more evident with each day. Note for example Bernard Lonergan's recent commentary on Thomas's identification of philosophic thinking with *understanding*, giving this word a new meaning and dimension. Thomas's also was a hospitable mind. In no sense a Platonist, his writings even so indicate that he incorporated Platonic thinking into his synthesis. Indeed his attitude toward other thinkers, even those with whom he disagreed sharply, is reported to have been, in general, one of extraordinary courtesy. Paradoxically enough, however, he believed with his fellow Dominicans that heretics must be suppressed. Heretics were then akin, in the popular estimation, to Communists in recent American history.

A reader who attempts for the first time to dig his way into the mammoth Summary of the Whole of Theology (*Summa totius philosophiae*) will naturally find it very difficult to cope with the Scholastic method, which, as has been indicated, states questions, cites a variety of opinions concerning them – often, indeed, offering some opportunity for defense and rebuttal – and then provides the answer which Thomas deemed correct. But it is possible for any modern reader to become quite fascinated with the discussion and to follow it with great interest even though a given topic may be remote from his experience.

At this point he will often be astonished to note that Thomas's thought and way of thinking are astonishingly contemporary with his own. This philosopher never wishes to be credulous. He is a resolute foe of everything which resembles superstition and refuses to endorse any proposed easy short cut to truth. Nevertheless he is not a rationalist in the usual sense of that term. He is determined not to put the comprehension of Reality into any strait jacket, is always willing to take into account the *mystery*, that is, the something human reason knows is there but cannot explore: How and why did the world come to be? How and why has man come into existence? These very fundamental questions no one can answer. Indeed it is the key to the thought and literature contemporary with ourselves that inability to respond is so frustrating that man's sole recourse is held to be despair blended with a stoic antidote to despair.

For Thomas the theological answer was clear, simple, and convincing. The Scriptures were inspired, were Revelation. They had been written, of course, against the sorry background of human experience, and so were manifestoes of sin and retribution. But they were also proclamations of the prayer which reveals continuing Divine affection. And what, when all was said and done, did the Scriptures say when the Old and New Testaments were fused into one? That God is Father, Son, and Holy Spirit; that the Triune Divine Being can be apprehended but not comprehended; and that the working of the Holy Spirit in our midst makes evident the continuing dominion of the Good in history through Christ.

Obviously the authenticity of Revelation thus set forth depends upon whether God can actually be apprehended. Since we cannot know Him, how can we find out that He exists? This question therefore became the central object of Thomas's theological concern. He did not deny that for some select persons it may well be possible to have an immediate, direct awareness of the Divine reality; but he strove to base his own awareness on reason ascending the ladder from sense experience to theological conclusions. Bernard Lonergan is surely correct in saying that Thomas's desire was not merely to establish the validity of Theism but also to make reasonable, assimilable, the riches of belief in the Trinity.

Since these are the fundamental quests of Thomistic theology they are also those which have been most widely discussed, accepted, and dissented from. To a reader who tries to cut his way through the argumentation it is often difficult to see how magnificent are the leaps of his genuinely poetic spirit into the dark. When, for example, one is told by Thomas (though the idea was not original with him) that the rational spirit in each human being is directly created by God, one loses oneself in a vision of a loving and yet determined act of Divine affection. When he suggests that a child conceived in a filthy embrace between a prostitute and a random lover nevertheless compels the finger of God to touch the embryo with a light that will eventually – though the born child might never realize it – bring it into a direct and immortal relationship with God, one may indeed be listening to an argument, but one has also been invited to share in a flash of insight which makes Creator and creature one. Blessed is he who can believe this, for it is on this conviction that the idea of human dignity eventually rests. How awesome, then, is the begetting of a child! Thomistic theology, even spelled out so prosaically, is as rich in its apprehension of Divine affection as is Dante's *Divina Commedia* itself. The great poem and the *Summa* are twin medieval miracles.

Did Thomas's effort to blend Aristotelianism with the New Testament succeed? In many respects the Catholic Church – which he served before knowing that as a result of religious reform movements, it would have to shape a definition of doctrine different from that of his day—

responded affirmatively. But the syntheses which he had so laboriously devised gave way to the later elaborate sophism of camp-followers of Scholasticism as well as to the Idealism of times closer to ourselves. It was not until the mid-nineteenth century that 'Thomism' was sponsored by a Pope as the 'official philosophy' of the Catholic Church. Until that time it had probably served Protestantism better, particularly in England.

On his way to the Second Council of Lyons, where another attempt would be made to heal the schism between the Churches of the East and West, Thomas died at the Abbey of Fossanova in the Campagna on March 7, 1274. Some months earlier he had a shattering mystical experience of what it would mean to live in eternal bliss; and so at last the poet in him superseded the logician. But however paltry all his disputation may have seemed to him as a result, it is this thinking through of things Divine and human which remains his distinctive legacy to mankind.

GEORGE N. SHUSTER

South Bend, Indiana

TABLE OF CONTENTS

❦ Song is the leap of mind in the eternal breaking out into sound.

❦ As dawn is the opening and dusk the close of the ordinary day, so the knowledge of the original being of things in the Word is described as the morning light, while the knowledge of them as they stand in their own natures is described as the evening light. The Word is the source, as it were, from which realities stream, flowing into the very being things have within themselves.

❦ Better to light up than merely to shine, to deliver to others contemplated truths than merely to contemplate.[1]

❦ In contemplation the mind is not at pause but fully active.[2]

❦ What a pity if philosophers, who are expected to be the chief seekers and lovers of truth and to see as much of it as can be seen by man, should decide after all that truth cannot be discovered. How they should then grieve that their studies have been all in vain.

1 From the argument that the perfect life is neither exclusively contemplative nor exclusively active.

2 *Active* and *productive* are not equivalent terms.

❧ What is false in nature is false from every point of view.

❧ A blacksmith should be a metallurgist, and a natural scientist should study the natures of stones and horses as pure meanings appearing in sensation. Nevertheless, a blacksmith who does not know how a ploughshare is used will be incompetent, and a natural scientist without feel for sensible qualities will not do justice to physical things.

❧ To strive for an end that cannot be secured is futile, and the hope of satisfaction there is illusory.

❧ Because philosophy arises from awe a philosopher is bound in his way to be a lover of myths and poetic fables. Poets and philosophers are alike in being big with wonder.

❧ When asked what he professed himself to be, Pythagoras was unlike his predecessors and would lay no claim to be a wise man, for to him that appeared presumptuous; he professed to be a philosopher, that is a lover of wisdom.

❧ Christian theology issues from the light of faith, philosophy from the natural light of reason. Philosophical truths cannot be opposed to the truths of faith, they fall short indeed, yet they also admit common analogies; and some moreover are foreshadowings, for nature is the preface to grace.

❧ What is natural cannot wholly perish.

❧ The divine rights of grace do not abolish the human rights of natural reason.

❧ Grace and virtue copy the order of nature instituted by divine wisdom.

❧ He learns who takes a meaning in the spirit of its utterance. The

Word of God the Father breathes love. A loving welcome is a condition of learning. *It moves into holy souls and makes saints and friends of God* (Wisd. vii. 27[1]).

❧ Truth is a divine thing, a friend more excellent than any human friend.

❧ The sun shines from outside us, but the sun of the mind, which is God, lights from within.

❧ All mutables bring us back to a first immutable.

❧ Perfect immortality implies complete immutability: as Augustine says, every change is a kind of death.

❧ Immutability is the strength of God.

❧ Stability is a necessary condition of happiness – as Aristotle remarks, we do not look upon the happy man as a kind of chameleon.

❧ Did eternal mind not exist then no truth would be eternal.

❧ If all created being were wiped out, the pure meaning of essence would still persist; if all human individuals were destroyed, rationality would still remain a predicate of human nature.

❧ The art of sailing governs the art of shipbuilding.

❧ Divinity is said to be the being of all things, not as their pith, but as their maker and exemplar cause.

❧ We praise God, not for his benefit, but for our own.

❧ Mingled things are more pleasing than simple things, a chord more so than a single bass or treble note.

[1] Biblical references throughout are to the Vulgate.

❧ Goodness and being are identical in reality, but the term *goodness* conveys what the term *being* does not, namely, the quality of being desirable.

❧ Augustine declares that nobody rightly uses God, for he is to be enjoyed. The last end is not a utility.

❧ What is worthy and what useful, is for the reason to decide; what is delightful is decided by the desire, which may not match the reason. Therefore every delight may not have moral goodness.

❧ Delight is not best just because it is delight, but because it is repose with the best.

❧ The good and the beautiful are the same in substance, for they are established on a single real form; but they are different in meaning, for the good answers to appetite and acts like a final cause, while the beautiful answers to knowledge and acts like a formal cause. Things are called beautiful which give delight on being seen.

❧ Three conditions of beauty–first, integrity or completeness, for broken things are ugly; second, due proportion and harmony; third, brightness and colour.

❧ Clearness and proportion go to compose the beautiful or handsome. Dionysius says that God is beautiful for he is the cause of the consonance and clearness of all things. Bodily beauty consists in well-shaped members with freshness of complexion; spiritual beauty, which is the same as honourable good, in fair dealing according to the candour of reason.

❧ The senses most charged with knowledge are the most set on beauty. The beautiful is the same as the good, but with a difference of accent. Good is what all desire; therefore is it of the essence of beauty that at the knowledge and sight of it the desire is stilled. The senses closest to mind, namely sight and hearing, are most engaged by beauty. We speak about beautiful sights and sounds, but not about beautiful tastes and smells. And so beauty adds to the meaning of goodness a relationship to the power of knowledge. The good is that which simply pleases desire, the beautiful that which pleases on being perceived.

Homes are not beautiful if they are empty. Things are beautiful by the indwelling of God.

Some seize on this as the difference between time and eternity, that time has beginning and end, but eternity not. This difference, however, is quite incidental and not essential; for even granting that time always was and always will be, there still remains this difference between them, that eternity is simultaneously whole, whereas time is not. Eternity is the measure of permanence; time the measure of change.

What is most strikingly certain is that the first cause surpasses human wit and speech. He knows God best who owns that whatever he thinks and says falls short of what God really is.

It may be said that in human affairs the same fate attends good and bad alike; *All things happen equally to the just and the wicked* (Eccles. ix. 2); and therefore that human affairs are not ruled by providence. It may indeed strike us that there is no rhyme or reason in the result because we are ignorant of the particulars of divine dispensation, yet we need have no doubt there is a good reason. A man goes into a smithy and judges that the tools are needlessly numerous, but that is because he has no knowledge of the craft, for they are all serviceable and are designed for a proper purpose.

As the impetus in the arrow's flight shows the archer's aim, so the spontaneous necessity of natural things declares the governance of divine providence.

God's spirit is said to move over the waters as an artist's will moves over the material to be shaped by his art.

❧ To hold creatures cheap is to slight divine power.

❧ Art, the idea of a thing to be made in the mind of the maker, is possessed most authentically by God. *Wisdom, which is the worker of all things, taught me* (Wisd. vii. 21). To give, not for any return but from the very excellence and consonance of giving, is an act of liberality. God is supremely liberal.

❧ Existence is all-pervading. When a particular man comes to be, what first appears is existence, then life, then humanity, for he is an animal before he is a man.[1] And so back again, he first loses the use of reason and life and breath remain, then he loses these, but existents are left.

❧ Every creature is to God as the air to the sun that lights it.

❧ The very differences that divide beings among themselves are real. God is not the author of the drift towards nothingness, but of being; he is the principle, not of fault, but of multitude.

❧ Many embarrassments crop up from the conclusion that no creatures take an active part in the production of natural effects. To begin with, if God alone operated, and none of them – bodies especially – were causes, variegation would not be found among their apparent effects, for it is not God who is modified through working in various things. Empirically you do not expect fire to freeze, or anything but a baby to be born from human parents. The causation of lower effects should not be so attributed to divine power as to abolish the causality of lower causes.

❧ Nothing appears more to impugn divine providence in human affairs than the affliction of the innocent.

❧ Though evil is neither good nor of God, nevertheless to understand it is both good and from God.

[1] The priority is in the arrangement of realities; a succession measurable by time is not alleged.

❦ Evil cannot be known simply as evil, for its core is hollow, and can be neither recognized nor defined save by the surrounding good.

❦ Evil precisely as such is not a reality in things, but a deprivation of some particular good inhering in a particular good.

❦ Through failing to free themselves from their imaginations, some have been unable to understand that anything can exist without being situated somewhere.

❦ To inquire into the meaning of animal is one business, to inquire into the meaning of human animal quite another.

❦ The principle of intellectual activity, which we term the human soul, is a bodiless and completely substantial principle.

This principle, also termed the mind or intellect, can act without the body having an intrinsic part in the activity. Nothing can act independently unless it be independent.

❦ The soul is part of time existing above time in eternity: it contains nature, but surpasses the physical principle of motion measured by time.

❦ Our body's substance is not from an evil principle, as the Manichees imagine, but from God. And therefore by the friendship of charity, by which we love God, should we cherish the body.

❦ *The flesh rejoices in the living God* (Ps. lxxxiii. 2 Vulgate), not by carnal activity reaching up to God, but by the overflowing of the heart, as when feeling follows willing.

❦ To be united to body is not to the detriment of soul, but for its enrichment. There is the substantial benefit of completing human nature, and the accidental benefit of achieving knowledge that can only be acquired through the senses.

❦ Man excels the other animals in the internal senses, but in some of the external senses he does not compare; thus his is the weakest sense of smell.

❦ Youth and age can be in the soul both at once, though not in the body; the former for alacrity, the latter for gravity.

❦ Nothing unnatural can be perpetual, and therefore the soul will not be without the body for ever.

❦ The habits of building and weaving and making music are in the soul and from the soul. But it is more accurate to say that the builder builds, and not that his art builds, though he builds through his art. So also it is better to say, not that the soul understands or feels pity, but that the man so acts through the soul.

❦ Knower and known are one principle of activity inasmuch as one reality results from them both, namely the mind in act. I say that one reality results, for herein mind is conjoined to thing understood, whether immediately or through a likeness. The knower as such is not an efficient or material cause, except on account of special conditions when knowledge may require action or passion.[1]

❦ Conceptions of heart and mind come forth in silence and without sound, but by audible words the silence of the heart is manifested.

❦ Through smell man enjoys the scent of lilies and roses; he finds them pleasing to him in themselves; whereas other animals take pleasure in smells – dogs, for instance – and colours only because they point to something else.

❦ Mental activity rises from sensation, yet in the very object of sense the mind perceives many notes that escape the senses.

[1] As when knowledge works through an organic process.

❧ In every good the supreme good is desired.

❧ All fear springs from love. Ordered love is included in every virtue, disordered love in every vice.

❧ Love is absolutely stronger than hate.

❧ Happiness is the greatest human good, the end to which all others are subordinate. It would be pernicious to a degree were happiness a matter of good luck, for then all other goods would be even more fortuitous, and so any deliberate attempt to lead a good life would go by the board.

❧ The desire for joy is inherently stronger than the fear of sadness, though under certain circumstances men's preoccupation may be with avoiding the latter rather than seeking the former.

❧ The dead can be honoured or disgraced, their descendants may be prosperous or unfortunate. And so happiness lies not even in the grave.

❧ Perfect enjoyment demands intelligence.

❧ The factors of happiness may be essential, antecedent, or consequent.

❧ The first mover and author of the universe is Mind, and therefore its ultimate purpose is the good of mind: and this is truth.

❧ Man's final happiness does not consist in moral activity, for it is ultimate and not subservient to a higher end, whereas moral activity is directed to something above itself. We may draw a comparison: a soldierly effort is subordinate to victory and peace; it is foolish to fight for the sake of fighting.

❧ No one can live without delight, and that is why a man deprived of spiritual joy goes over to carnal pleasures.

❧ Delight perfects happiness as beauty does youth.

❧ The voluptuous life places its end in carnal pleasure which is common to us and brutes; the taste is slavish, the life all very well for a beast.

❧ Men alone take pleasure in the very beauty itself of sensible things; their faces uplifted, not downcast.

❧ Hell is ruled by time, not by true eternity.

❧ The proximate rule is the human reason, the supreme measure is the eternal law.

❧ Every judgement of conscience, be it right or wrong, be it about things evil in themselves or morally indifferent, is obligatory, in such wise that he who acts against his conscience always sins.

❧ What is dictated by a mistaken conscience is not consonant with the law of God, nevertheless it is construed as the law of God, and therefore, simply speaking, if a man goes against it he contravenes the law of God.

❧ The inquiry, *whether the will that obeys a mistaken conscience is right*, is equivalent to, *whether a mistaken conscience is any excuse*:

If the reason or conscience is mistaken through voluntary error, either directly wished or tolerated by negligence, about what one is bound to know, then such an error does not absolve the will from blame. But it is an excuse if the error causing the non-voluntary wrong follows from ignorance of some circumstance without any negligence. For example, if a mistaken reason bids a man sleep with another man's wife, to do this will be evil if based on ignorance of a divine law he ought to know; but if the misjudgement is occasioned by thinking that the woman is really his own wife, and she wants him and he wants her, then his will is free from fault.

❧ Pleasure lies in being, not becoming.

❧ The worth of virtue shines out when a man readily bears many and grievous blows of misfortune: not that he is insensitive to pain and sadness, as the Stoics urged, but that he remains manly and great-hearted, and upright in his reason.

❧ Love is the form, mover, and root of the virtues.

❧ By and large every virtue is magnificent.

❧ Virtue is a good habit.

❧ Complete characters do not take scandal.

❧ Virtue has three effects; it removes evil, works for good, and disposes to the best.

❧ Among objects in themselves lovable, some are loved solely for themselves and never for anything else – thus happiness which is the last end – while others are loved both for their own sake, in that they possess some intrinsic worth, and also because they serve the purpose of conveying us to a more perfect good – thus are the virtues lovable.

❧ Prudence excepted, intellectual virtue can exist without moral virtue.

❧ Art is the right idea of things to be made; their goodness does not depend on the disposition of the human appetite, but on the fact that the workmanship is sound. The merit of an artist is judged by the quality of his work; his state of will is irrelevant. Here art is like the theoretical habits of mind, which are concerned with what things are in themselves, not with our reactions to them. Pleasant humour or spleen makes no difference to a mathematical demonstration. Art is a virtue in the same sense; it does not ensure the right use of a thing, for this is proper to moral virtue.

❧ Goodwill is required for a man to use his art aright, and this is induced by moral virtue.

❧ The value of art consists, not in the artist, but in the work of art, for making, which is an action going out into external material, is a perfection, not of the maker, but of the thing made. But the value of prudence is in the doer, who is perfected by his activity, for prudence is the right idea of deeds to be done.

❧ The gate to human life hinges on the cardinal virtues. The contemplative life is superhuman, the life of sensual pleasure beastly, but the active life is properly human, and human activity turns on the practice of the moral virtues.

❧ Prudence essentially possesses reasonable good, justice makes it, courage and temperance preserve it.

❧ The chief effective control of human activity is provided by prudence. Virtue springs from man's inner composure, but no less important is his bearing to other people, and here his intercourse is adjusted by justice. His poise when faced with the onset of passion for the pleasures of touch is assured by temperance, and when he would shrink from great perils courage makes him stand intrepid even before the danger of death.

❧ The theologian considers sin mainly as an offence against God; the moral philosopher as contrary to reasonableness.

❧ There is evil, and there is also something from which evil may follow. In the first respect God cannot be feared, since he is goodness itself. In the second respect he may be feared because from him, or with reference to him, some evil may come our way; the evil of punishment respectively and the evil of fault when we are separated from him.

❧ If a man cleaves to God through fear of punishment it will be servile fear; if through fear of offending him it will be filial fear.

❧ Sin falls short of the wisdom and prudence that should be in charge of what we do. Therefore a bad man is an ignorant man.

❧ Though nobody is foolish by choice, we may will the things from which foolishness follows.

❧ The worse the vice the better always the opposite virtue.

❧ Well-ordered self-love is right and natural.

❧ Vice cannot entirely destroy the capacity and aptness for grace.

❧ The desire for good is more corrupted than is the knowledge of truth.

❧ To speak of unforgivable sin is to impugn divine power.

❧ The order of divine justice does not treat those who are still travellers as though they had arrived. Now to be in an unchangeable state, either of good or of evil, is the end; whereas wayfaring is our present condition, as is evidenced by the mutability of body and soul. Divine justice, therefore, does not require that a man after falling into sin should lie there for ever.

❧ Knowledge is achieved by the thing known being united through its meaning to the knower. But the effect of love is that the thing itself is somehow united to the lover.

❧ Gratitude tries to return more than has been received.

❧ Heroic or divine virtue does not differ from the normal run of virtue except by its more perfect mode of activity, and because it disposes to values higher than those generally accessible. It is virtue above the usual course, called by Plotinus a certain sublime manner of virtue, and attributed to the purified soul.

❧ The visitation of the Lord may be for condemnation, for correction, for consolation.

❧ Grace does not destroy nature but completes it. Hence the natural reason subserves faith as the natural desire of will is the undercurrent of charity.

❧ Wonder is a kind of desire in knowing. It is the cause of delight because it carries the hope of discovery.

❧ Wonder is impossible without reason, for it implies a comparing of effect and cause.

❧ There are various kinds of silence; of dullness, of security, of patience, of a quiet heart.

❧ Believers do not lightly believe truths the human reason cannot verify experimentally. *We have not followed cunningly devised fables* (2 Pet. i. 16).

❧ Hopelessness about eternal life may come either because heaven is not accounted for much, or because it is reckoned impossible to obtain. Spiritual goods do not strike us as very valuable when our affections are sapped by love of bodily pleasures, and especially sexual pleasures. By craving these a man comes to feel distaste for spiritual values. Thus, despair is caused by lust. We are also led to imagine that this noble prize is beyond our reach by an excessive dejection into which we sink and from which we feel we shall never be extricated. Thus spiritual boredom generates despair.

❧ Between friends there is no need of justice properly so called. They share everything in common. A friend is an *alter ego*, and a man does not have justice towards himself. Let two men be together; justice is not enough, for something more is required, namely friendship.

❧ It is of the nature of friendship not to be hidden; otherwise it would only be a kind of well-wishing.

❦ You cannot make friends with people whose company and conversation you do not enjoy – with people, for instance, who are harsh, quarrelsome, and addicted to back-biting. Crusty old men may be benevolent in that they wish well and will do good at a pinch, but they are not truly friendly, for they do not share their lives and rejoice together in the company of friends.

❦ To rejoice and to be sad on the same grounds is the sign of sharing.

❦ Friendship is love simply speaking; desire is love in a qualified sense.

❦ Love is a binding force, by which another is joined to me and cherished as myself.

❦ By loving God a man glows to gaze on his beauty.

❦ The lover is not content with superficial knowledge of the beloved, but strives for intimate discovery and entrance.

❦ By peace a man is single-minded in himself and of one mind with others.

❦ Peace is opposed to conflict within oneself, as well as to conflict with others outside.

❦ Solitude is like poverty, an instrument for perfection, not its essence. To embark on a solitary life without proper training beforehand is very risky.

❦ The effects of love should be shown as well as felt.

❦ The man to be elected should be the best man for the task, not necessarily the person with the finest character, or the most full of charity.

❧ It may happen that a man who is less devout or learned may serve the common good better because of his energy or capacity for taking pains or something of the sort.

❧ In human affairs there is the common good, the well-being of the state or nation; there is also a human good which does not lie in the community, but is personal to each man in himself; not, however, that it is privately profitable to the exclusion of others.

❧ Personality means completeness, not necessarily particularity in a common nature.

❧ No possession is joyous without a companion.

❧ *Every man at the beginning doth set forth good wine, but thou hast kept the good wine until now* (John ii. 10). The tale points the moral. For a tempter begins by alluring, and shows his hand only when his victims are drunk: *it comes in sweetly, but at the last it biteth like an adder* (Prov. xxiii. 31). Then again, a convert may begin well, but afterwards falls away: *are ye so foolish? Having begun in the Spirit, are ye now made perfect by the flesh?* (Gal. iii. 3).

❧ But burdensome and bitter may be the start with Christ: *strait is the gate and narrow the way which leads to life* (Matt. vii. 20). Then as we grow in faith and sound doctrine our movements become more lissom and easy: *when thou goest thy steps shall not be straitened, and when thou runnest thou shall not stumble* (Prov. iv. 12). All who will devoutly follow Christ must suffer hardship and grief to begin with: *amen, amen I say to you that ye shall weep and lament* (John xvi. 20). Afterwards come peace and joy: *your sorrow shall be turned into joy* (John xvi. 20). *The sufferings of this present time are not to be compared with the glory that shall be revealed in us* (Gal. viii. 8).

❧ The sight of an effect rouses a natural desire to know the cause. The human mind can view the whole range of things, and therefore instinctively craves to know their cause, which, ultimately, is God alone. Happiness is not attained until this natural appetite is at rest. Not any sort of understanding will do; only divine understanding will satisfy; only knowing God will produce the state where restlessness is stilled.

❧ Human philosophy examines creatures as elements of this world. Christian faith, however, does not stop short there; fire is taken, not as fire, but as representing the divine majesty and beckoning us to God: *the glory of the Lord shines through all his creation; how should his faithful servant herald his marvels enough?* (Ecclus. xiii. 17). A philosopher and a theologian pursue different interests; one looks for inherently natural characteristics, the other for relations opening out to God. Even when they look at the same thing their point of view is different. The philosopher starts from proximate causes, the theologian from the first cause as divinely revealed; his concern is the manifestation of God's omnipotence and glory.

❧ The gifts of grace are added to us in order to enhance the gifts of nature, not to take them away. The native light of reason is not obliterated by the light of faith gratuitously shed on us. Mere reasoning can never discover the truths which faith perceives; on the other hand, it cannot discover any disagreement between its own intrinsically natural truths and those divinely revealed. Were there any contradiction, one set or the other would be fallacious, and, since both are from God, he would be the author of our deception, which is out of the question. In fact the imperfect reflects the perfect; our enterprise should be to draw out the analogies between the discoveries of reason and the commands of faith.

❧ The first cause defies description. There is a different turn of meaning about statements which say that God is this or that and statements which attribute qualities to the things around us. The divine being is beyond our ways of making sense of things. Dionysius remarks that negative statements about God can be accurate, but the affirmative statements are clumsy and halting.

❦ *Knowledge puffs up* (Cor. viii. 1): the text applies when science is without love.

❦ God so lives that he has no principle of life.

❦ God's love for things is better than ours. For our will is not the cause of goodness, but responds to goodness. Our liking does not produce the good of the thing we love: it is the other way round – the goodness, real or apparent, of the thing calls forth our love, whether that love be a love which rests content with its object as it finds it or a love which seeks to improve it. But God's love, which makes things out of nothingness, impregnates all the goodness they have.

❦ Love can be greater or less on the side either of the lover or the beloved. With respect to the will's activity, loving is said to be more or less intense: here God does not love some more than others, for he loves all with a single and simple act, unvarying and perpetual. With respect to the object, we are said to love more – though not necessarily with greater vehemence – where there is more to love: here God loves some more than others. The conclusion is forced on us, for otherwise, since his will is the cause of goodness, some things would not be better than others.

❦ Goodness is generous. God is supremely good. Therefore supremely generous. But he cannot supremely give himself to creatures, for they cannot receive his entire goodness. The perfect gift of himself is not to another diverse by nature. Therefore within him there is distinctiveness without division.

Sheer joy is his, and this demands companionship.

Perfect love must be matched. Charity is unselfish love. But creatures cannot be loved above all. Therefore in the divine begetting there is the perfect lover and perfect beloved, distinct but of one nature.

❦ The Incarnate Word is like a word of speech. For as sensible sounds express what we think so Christ's body manifests the Eternal Word.

❧ Evil as such cannot be desired.

❧ History recounts that a vestal virgin carried water from the Tiber in a perforated pitcher without spilling a drop, a holding back of natural flow comparable to the stopping of the Jordan. Therefore, some have concluded, demons can work miracles.

I reply that it would not be at all strange if the true God worked this miracle to commend chastity. The old pagan virtues were from God. If it was not divinely done, then no miracle took place: spirits, in point of fact, can locally stir or stay the flow of fluids by their natural power.

❧ Miracles lessen the merit of faith to the extent that they argue an unwillingness to believe the Scriptures, a hardness of heart that demands signs and wonders. All the same, it is better for men to turn to the Faith because of miracles than to remain altogether in the state of unbelief.

❧ The essence of virtue consists in the doing rather of what is good than of what is difficult.

❧ We are committed to the belief that the blessed see God's very being. Happiness is the ultimate achievement of rational nature. A thing is finally complete when it attains its original purpose, and without being forced. I add that qualification, because a thing reaches God by what it is and not by what it does. First, by likeness. This is common to every creature, and the rule is that the closer the likeness to God the more the excellence. Second by activity – I leave aside the singular personal union of man and God in Christ – by which I mean the rational creature's activity of knowing and loving God.

Man's soul comes directly from God, and therefore finds its happiness by returning directly to God. He must be seen for what he is in himself; seen, that is, without a medium which acts as a likeness and representation of the thing known, such as a sense-image in the eye or a reflection in a mirror, but not without a medium called the light of glory, which strengthens the mind to have this vision.

Some have taught that the first object of knowledge even in this life is God himself who is the first truth, and that through him everything else is known.[1] Others have professed what is less obviously unwarranted, that the divine essence, though not in itself the original object of consciousness, is yet the light in which everything is seen. Yet they cannot be supported. To begin with, the light divinely shed within us is the natural light of our intelligence, which is not the first object of knowledge, either as regards its nature, for elaborate analysis is required to know the nature of mind, or as regards its existence, for we do not perceive that we have an intelligence except when we perceive that we are understanding something else. Nobody knows that he is knowing save in knowing something else, and consequently the knowledge of an intelligible object precedes intellectual self-consciousness.

The existence of God and similar truths about him attainable by strict rationalism are not articles of faith, but preambles to them. Faith presupposes natural knowledge, even as grace presupposes nature, and perfection the capacity for it. Nevertheless there is nothing to prevent a man from accepting as an article of belief something that can be scientifically known and demonstrated, though perchance not by him.

[1] A doctrine commonly called ontologism.

❦ Whether God's existence[1] is self-evident. . . . We advance on this point as follows.[2]

It appears to be self-evident that God exists. For those truths are self-evident about which our knowledge is innate. Now, as Damascene says, the knowledge that God exists is implanted naturally in all men.

Moreover, those truths are called self-evident which are at once assented to when the meaning of their terms is recognized. When we know the meaning of *whole* and *part* we instantly agree that every whole is greater than any one of its parts. Well then, as soon as we grasp the meaning of this term *God* we are bound to see immediately that his existence is implied. For it signifies that than which nothing greater can be conceived. Now what exists really as well as mentally is greater than what exists merely in our mind. When the term *God* is understood, an object with mental existence is present which must also be credited with existence in reality. Therefore that God exists is a self-evident proposition.[3]

Moreover, the existence of truth is self-evident. The denial that truth exists is an assertion that truth does not exist, and this, if well-founded, is itself a true proposition. If anything be true, then truth must exist. But God is truth. Therefore his existence is self-evident.

But on the contrary: nobody can conceive the opposite of what is self-evident. The denial of God's existence can, however, be entertained by the mind. Therefore his existence is not self-evident.

I give judgement by saying: a truth can be self-evident in two manners, in itself but not to us, or in itself and to us as well. A proposition is

[1] *Deum esse*, that God is. The usual sense of *existing* as meaning being established *extra causas*, or as we might say, past undoing, does not apply to God who has no cause. Yet it is easier to speak of his existence than of his is-ness. So *esse* when it stands for ultimate substantial actuality has been translated as *existence* or *existing*. Even in the case of creatures, these terms are too meagre and adventitious to stand for what St. Thomas meant by *esse*; yet they seem preferable to the vaguer *being* or even *actual being*, and to the more pedantic *is-ness*.

[2] An article of the *Summa Theologica* is here set out in full. It shows the typical structure of 1. *Title*, which advances an open question ('Whether, &c.'); 2. *Objections* ('It appears, &c.'); 3. *Sed Contra* ('But on the contrary, &c.'); 4. *Body of the Article* ('I give judgement that, &c.'); 5. *Replies to the objections* ('To the first, &c.').

[3] The famous Anselmic argument from the *Proslogion*.

self-evident when the predicate is contained in the very notion of the subject. If, therefore, the meaning of both subject and predicate be well recognized the proposition will be unanimously admitted, as in the case of the first principles of thought where the terms, such as being, non-being, whole, part, and the like, express hackneyed notions with which everybody is familiar. But to those who are unacquainted with the meaning of its subject and predicate, a proposition, though indeed evident in itself, may not so appear; as Boethius says, some notions are commonplaces and self-evident only to experts, for instance that incorporeal things do not occupy place. I declare then that this proposition, *God exists*, though of itself self-evident – since subject and predicate are identical, for God is his existence, as will be shown hereafter – is nevertheless not self-evident to us, because we do not know what the essence of God is; it requires to be demonstrated by truths more evident to us though less evident in themselves, namely by his effects.

To the first objection: an undifferentiated knowledge that God exists is implanted by nature, for he is the health we instinctively desire, and what we naturally desire that also we somehow know. But this does not amount to a knowledge of God's existing as such, any more than to know that somebody is approaching is to know Peter, though in fact it is Peter. For there are many who imagine that man's perfect good, or bliss, lies in riches or pleasures or something of the sort.

To the second objection: he who hears this term *God* perchance may not understand it to signify that than which nothing greater can be conceived. Some have thought that God was a body. But granting that everybody accepts the term in this sense, it still does not follow that something existing in reality is entailed, or anything more than an object of mind. Nor can we urge that it must exist in reality, unless we concede that there is in reality a being than which nothing greater can be thought of, and this is not assumed by those who deny the existence of God.

To the third objection: the existence of abstract truth in general is self-evident, but the existence of a primary true thing is not self-evident as far as we are concerned.

❧ It may be argued that God does not exist. For if one of two contraries is unbounded its opposite is altogether ousted. But the word *God* means that he is existing infinite goodness. Were he to exist no evil could remain. But we come across evil in the world. Therefore he does not exist.

Moreover, explanations should be economical.[1] It seems that everything that appears in the world can be accounted for on the supposition that God does not exist. Natural processes can be resolved solely into physical determinism, and design can be resolved solely into the factors of human reason or will. There is no need then to postulate the existence of God.

But on the contrary, God said in person, *I am who am* (Exod. iii. 14).

I explain by saying that the existence of God can be proved in five ways. . . .

☙ The first and most open way is presented by change or motion.[2] It is evident to our senses and certain that in the world some things are in motion.

Whatever is in motion is set in motion by another. For nothing is in motion unless it be potential to that to which it is in motion; whereas a thing sets in motion inasmuch as it is actual, because to set in motion is naught else than to bring a thing from potentiality to actuality, and from potentiality a subject cannot be brought except by a being that is actual; actually hot makes potentially hot become actually hot, as when fire changes and alters wood. Now for the same thing to be simultaneously and identically actual and potential is not possible, though it is possible under different respects; what is actually hot cannot simultaneously be potentially hot, though it may be potentially cold. It is impossible, therefore, for a thing both to exert and to suffer motion in the same respect and according to the same motion.

If that which sets in motion is itself in motion then it also must be set in motion by another, and that in its turn by another again. But here we cannot proceed to infinity, otherwise there would be no first mover, and consequently no other mover, seeing that subsequent movers do not

[1] Ockam's Razor was a truism long before the fourteenth century.

[2] Motion, movement, change, *motus*, are synonymous throughout. Note, the argument is not restricted to local motion.

initiate motion unless they be moved by a former mover, as stick by hand.

Therefore we are bound to arrive at the first mover set in motion by no other, and this everyone understands to be God.

❦ Having indicated that the attempt to prove God's existence is not hopeless from the outset, we proceed now to fix on the arguments of philosophers and theologians alike, beginning with Aristotle who sets off from the concept of change. His argument takes two directions, of which the first is as follows.

Everything in a process of change is set in motion by another. Our senses tell us that things are in motion, the sun for instance. Therefore they are set in motion by another. Now this setter-in-motion is either itself in motion or it is not. If not, then we have our conclusion, namely the necessity of inferring a motionless mover which we term God. But if it is itself in motion then it must be set in motion by another. Either we have an infinite series or we arrive at a changeless mover. But we cannot go back infinitely. Therefore we must infer a first changeless mover.

There are two propositions to be proved; first, that everything in motion is set in motion by another; second, that an infinite series of things setting and set in motion is impossible.

❦ Note that Plato, who says that movers are in motion, takes the term *motion* in a wider sense than does Aristotle who keeps to its narrowest sense, meaning the actuality still potential of a subject in potentiality, which applies only to quantified and corporeal reality. Whenever Plato speaks of a thing that moves itself not being a body he includes in motion such operations as understanding and thinking. In other contexts Aristotle also adopts this usage, as when he speaks of the first mover moving itself by understanding and willing and loving itself. There is no embarrassment here, for it amounts to the same whether with Plato we arrive at the first thing that moves itself or with Aristotle at the first thing that is altogether motionless.

❧ The second approach starts from the nature of efficient causality.[1] Among phenomena we discover an order of efficient causes. But we never come across, nor ever shall, anything that is an efficient cause of itself; such a thing would be prior to itself, which is impossible. It is also impossible to go on to infinity with efficient causes, for in an ordered series[2] the first is the cause of the intermediate and the intermediate is the cause of the last. Whether or not the intermediate causes be one or many is irrelevant. Take away the cause and the effect also goes. Therefore if there were not a first among efficient causes – which would be the case in an infinite series – there would be no intermediate causes nor an ultimate effect. This plainly is not the case. A first cause, generally termed God, must therefore be inferred.

❧ The intervening causes may be one or many, but the conclusion is not affected. If they be many, then they are all classed together as possessing the character of being intermediaries. Similarly it makes no difference whether they be limited in number or infinite, for so long as they are intermediate causes they never possess the character of a first cause.

If efficient causes were imagined as stretching to infinity it would follow that all causes would be intermediate. For in general one is bound to say that all parts in any infinite system of magnitude or causality must be middle parts, otherwise one part would be first and another part last; both notions are irreconcilable with the infinite, which excludes every limit, either of beginning or of end.

❧ An infinite series of efficient causes in essential subordination is impossible. Causes essentially required for the production of a determinate effect cannot consequently be infinitely multiplied, as if a block could be shifted by a crowbar, which in turn is levered by a hand, and so on to infinity.

But an infinite series of causes in accidental subordination is not

[1] The argument follows the plan of the *prima via*, but deepens to include the being as well as the becoming of the realities about us.

[2] That is a series in essential subordination, or causes depending on another for their causality. The argument abstracts from whether or not a series in accidental subordination, or of events in succession, need ever be closed.

reputed impossible, so long as all the causes thus multiplied are grouped as one cause and their multiplication is incidental to the causality at work. For instance a blacksmith may work with many hammers because one after another breaks in his hand, but that one particular hammer is used after another particular one is incidental. Similarly that in begetting a child a man was himself begotten by another man; for he is father as man, not as son. In a genealogy of efficient causes all men have the same status of particular generator. Hence, for such a line to stretch back to infinity is not unthinkable.

❦ Man's natural reason tells him that he is under a higher power because of the deficiencies he feels in himself crying out for care and comfort. Whatever that higher may be, it is what all men term God.

❦ We observe in our environment how things are born and die away; they may or may not exist; to be or not to be – they are open to either alternative. All things cannot be so contingent, for what is able not to be may be reckoned as once a non-being, and were everything like that once there would have been nothing at all. Now were this true, nothing would ever have begun, for what is does not begin to be except because of something which is, and so there would be nothing even now. This is clearly hollow. Therefore all things cannot be might-not-have-beens; among them must be being whose existence is necessary.[1]

❦ Necessary reality is always actual; it is never poised between existence and non-existence. It is primary, and were it to disappear nothing would remain.

❦ Everything that is a possible-to-be has a cause, since its essence as such is equally uncommitted to the alternatives of existing and not existing. If it be credited with existence, then this must be from some cause. Causality, however, is not an infinite process. Therefore a necessary being is the conclusion. The principle of its necessity is either from outside or not. If not, then the being is inwardly necessary. If necessity

[1] The argument derives from Avicenna, *Metaphysics*.

comes from without, we must still propose a first being necessary of itself, since we cannot have an endless series of derivatively necessary beings.

❦ Substances are the primary realities. Destroy what is primary and everything else goes as well. Were all substances mortal and none of them everlasting, nothing would be permanent and everything would be transient. This is inconceivable.

❦ The fourth argument is taken from the degrees of reality we discover in things. Some are truer and better and nobler than others, so also with other perfections.[1] But more or less are attributed to different things in proportion as they variously approach something which is the maximum. Hence, there is something truest, and best, and noblest, and in consequence the superlative being, for the greatest truths are the greatest beings. Now the maximum in any order is the cause of all the other realities of that order. Therefore there is a real cause of being and goodness and all perfections whatsoever in everything; and this we term God.

❦ Above the human mind there must be set a higher mind, from which our mind receives its powers of understanding. To that which shares and which is mutable and imperfect there must always be presupposed that which is perfect essentially and which is unchanging and perfect. The human spirit is called intellectual by sharing in intellectual power. A sign thereof is that the human spirit is partially and not wholly intellectual; also that it comes to an understanding of truth by research and discussion; also that it enjoys imperfect understanding, for it does not understand everything, and even if it did there would have been a transition from potentiality. Therefore some higher mind must exist to kindle our soul into understanding.

❦ Another proof, taken from the governance of things, is introduced by Damascene and mentioned by Averroes. Contrary and discordant

[1] The argument applies only to analogical perfections, forms admitting more or less within themselves, not to fixed or univocal meanings differentiated from without. All strictly metaphysical concepts are analogical.

elements, it runs, cannot always, or nearly always, work harmoniously together unless they be directed by something providing each and all with their tendencies to a definite end. Now in the universe we see things of diverse natures conspiring together in one scheme, not rarely or haphazardly, but approximately always or for the most part. There must be something, therefore, whose providence directs the universe.[1]

❦ We observe that things without consciousness, such as physical bodies, operate with a purpose, as appears from their co-operating invariably, or almost so, in the same way in order to obtain the best result. Clearly then they reach this end by intention and not by chance. Things lacking knowledge move towards an end only when directed by someone who knows and understands, as an arrow by an archer. There is consequently an intelligent being who directs all natural things to their ends; and this being we call God.

❦ When diverse things are co-ordinated the scheme depends on their directed unification, as the order of battle of a whole army hangs on the plan of the commander-in-chief. The arrangement of diverse things cannot be dictated by their own private and divergent natures; of themselves they are diverse and exhibit no tendency to make a pattern. It follows that the order of many among themselves is either a matter of chance or it must be resolved into one first planner who has a purpose in mind. What comes about always, or in the great majority of cases, is not the result of accident. Therefore the whole of this world has but one planner or governor.

[1] Two distinct arguments, of which the second is independent, are engaged in the *quinta via*. The first is the argument from design, based on the concept of external finality, that is the arrangement of different things in a working pattern. The second is the argument from purpose, based on the concept of internal finality, the rationalization of any activity in the light of an end which, at the last analysis, is intellectually appointed.

THE PROBLEM OF EVIL

❦ There is not one first principle of evil as there is of good. In the first place, the original principle of things is essential good. Nothing can be essentially bad. Every being as being is good; evil does not exist except in a good subject.

In the second place, the first principle of good things is supreme and perfect good containing all goodness in itself. Now there cannot be a supreme evil, for though evil lessens good, it can never totally destroy good; while good remains, nothing can be an entire and unmitigated evil. For this reason Aristotle observes that a wholly evil thing would be self-destructive. Were all good entirely destroyed–and this would be required for evil to be complete–evil itself would vanish since its subject, namely good, would no longer be there.

In the third place, the very notion of evil is irreconcilable with the notion of a first principle, because evil is caused by good; also because evil can be a cause only incidentally, and therefore cannot be the first cause, since the accidental is subsequent to the essential.

Some have proclaimed that the two prime rulers are Good and Evil. Here lies a root of error from which other strange doctrines of the ancients have sprouted. In attending to the particular causes of particular effects they failed to consider the universal cause of all being. When they found one thing by its natural force injurious to another, they reckoned that the very nature of the thing was evil; as if one were to say that the nature of fire is evil because it burns down the house of some poor man. The estimate, however, of a thing's goodness does not primarily depend on any particular reference, but on its being and on its relation to the whole universe, wherein every part holds its perfectly appointed place.

Similarly, when they discovered two contrary particular causes of two contrary particular effects they were at a loss how to resolve them into a universal common cause; therefore they pushed back the contrariness of causes into the first principles of things. Since all contraries have a common ground, we should instead look for one common cause above their proper contrary causes.

❧ The devil is called the god of this world, not because he created it, but because worldlings serve him. St. Paul uses the same turn of phrase: *Whose god is their belly* (Phil. iii. 19).

❧ Since evil is deprivation and defect, and since defect can occur not only within a thing's natural condition but also in its dynamism as directed to an end, it follows that evil can have this double sense, namely of a deficiency of being, thus blindness is an organic defect, and of a deficiency of activity, thus limping is a functional defect. This evil in an activity, either physical or voluntary, which is not ordered to its appropriate end is called *peccatum*, or sin.[1] So a doctor sins in his action when he does not operate for health, so also does nature sin in begetting a monster.

❧ Evil is privation of good. Good is actuality, and this is double; primary actuality, which is the form and integrity of a thing, and secondary actuality, which is its operation. The incidence of evil is on both; on the former by a withdrawal of form or of any integral part, thus blindness or the lack of a limb; on the latter by a gap in the proper activity, either by non-performance or failure in execution or direction.

Now since good for its own sake is the proper object of will, the evil of being deprived of it has a special relevance to rational creatures endowed with will. The evil which consists in the impairment of form and

[1] Yet unless otherwise qualified by the context sin means moral disorder or fault, that is misdirection as regards man's ultimate happiness.

integrity has the characteristic of penalty or pain; the evil which consists in bad operations has the characteristic of fault, for it is imputed to someone as a fault when he falls short in his proper and responsible activity.

❧ We must say that every evil in some way has a cause. For evil is the deficiency of a good that is a thing's birthright. That anything falls short of its due and natural perfection can come about only from some cause dragging it out of its course.

Yet only what is good can cause. If we consider the various kinds of cause, the efficient, final, and formal causes, all spell a certain finish, which is a characteristic note of good; matter also, as being potential to good, verges on the nature of good. That good is the material cause of evil has already appeared. As regards the formal cause, evil has none; instead it is rather the privation of form. Similarly, it has no final cause, but is rather the privation of due order to end; good covers not only the end, but also the means. Evil has an efficient cause; this, however, is indirect, not direct.

Let us make this clearer by observing the difference of causation as regards evil in the action and as regards evil in the effect respectively. In the action evil is caused by defect of some active principle, either in the principal or in the instrumental cause; an ungainly walk may result either from a defect of motive power, as in babies, or from a disability of the limb, as in the lame. On the other hand, evil is caused in the effect sometimes by the very energy of the agent – not, however, in the proper effect of the agent – and sometimes by the intractability of the matter. When the privation of one form is a necessary consequence of the form introduced by the agent, as when fire expels the form of air or water, the more energetic the agent the more forcibly it impresses itself and destroys the contrary. Destruction comes then from the very strength of the flames; even so the energy is directly bent on mastering, not on destroying, though in effect it is incidentally destructive. But if there be a defect in the proper effect of fire, if, for instance, it fails to heat, then this is either because of weakness in the action, which throws us back on the defective principle already referred to, or from unsuitableness in the material, which does not receive the action of the flame playing on it.

But the fact that a thing is deficient is incidental to the goodness by which it is active. Hence, it is true to say that evil has naught but an incidental cause; in this sense good is the cause of evil.

❧ However greatly multiplied, evils can never consume the whole of good.

❧ To make this clear we should distinguish three headings of good: the first is precisely that good totally taken away by evil, namely the good attacked by evil; thus the light lost in darkness and the sight in blindness. The second is the good neither totally destroyed nor yet even lessened, namely the good which is the subject of evil; for example, the substance of air undiminished by darkness. The third is the good which is diminished but not destroyed, and this is the ability of the subject to act in the proper fashion.

Now this diminution should be illustrated by comparison with the slackening of qualities and forms, not with the subtraction of quantities. This slackening of ability may be tested by its contrary intensity. Ability grows more intense by dispositions toning the active faculty; the more multiplied the acts, the readier the subject becomes to receive the perfection and form of activity. And conversely, the more weakened the subject becomes by contrary dispositions induced by repeated and strong contrary acts, the slacker grows the power for right activity.

But even were the contrary disposition piled up indefinitely, the aptness for right action would be but indefinitely weakened, not wholly destroyed. The root would always remain, namely the substance of the subject. If you interposed an infinity of opaque screens between the air and the sun you would immeasurably diminish the lucidity of air, but this quality would not be destroyed so long as air remained, which of its nature is transparent. Similarly, even if sins could be piled up infinitely, and the soul's ability for gracious activity thereby infinitely lessened (for sins are like obstacles interposed between us and God, *our sins have separated between us and God* [Isa. lix. 2]), nevertheless, the aptness for virtue would not be totally destroyed, for it follows from the very nature of the soul.

❧ The capital of human nature diminished by sin is the natural inclination to virtue instinctive in man as a rational being; to act aright is to act according to reason. Now sin cannot destroy man's rationality altogether, for then he would no longer be capable of sin.

To illustrate a continuous diminution an example has been drawn from quantity. A given quantity can be infinitely subtracted from and yet never wholly disappear. Aristotle says that if you continuously take away the same quantity from a given amount it will eventually disappear, for instance if you keep on taking away a handsbreadth; but if instead the subtraction is always according to the same proportion, you can go on for ever, for instance if you halve what you start with, then again halve a half, and so on: what is subtracted is always less than what was subtracted just before. But this does not apply to the present case, for a later sin does not less diminish the virtue of nature than does a preceding one, but if anything rather more, especially if it be graver.

Therefore we must illustrate the situation otherwise. The inclination to virtue should be taken as a kind of intermediate reality between two extreme terms; on one side supported by and rooted in rational nature, and on the other side climbing to the achievement of virtue as to its finish and end. Weakening may affect either side. But sin does not strike at the root, since it does not diminish nature itself: what it does is to block the ability from reaching its end; the disability consists in the interposition of a barrier. Thus there can be an infinite lessening of virtue, for always another layer can be added, as when man piles sin on sin. Yet the instinct for right action always remains radically intact.

A
Ω

The essence of God is his existence. Moses was taught this sublime truth when he asked: *If the children of Israel say to me, what is his name; what shall I answer them?* The Lord replied: *I am who am; so shalt thou say to the children of Israel: he who is has sent me to you* (Exod. iii. 13–14).

Since there is no composition of quantitative parts in God, for he is not a body; nor a composition of matter and form; nor are his nature and complete substantiality distinct; nor his essence and existence; nor is there a composition of genus and difference; nor of subject and accidents–it is plain that God is altogether simple and nowise composite.

The plurality of names for divine perfections does not militate against divine simplicity. Perfections which are diversified in other things by different forms exist in God by identical virtue. An analogy may be drawn from the faculties of knowing. The single ability of mind knows all things which the sensibility knows by diverse abilities–and many other things besides. Every kind of perfection, which other things obtain only in varied diversity, is possessed by God in his own single and simple being–yea and many more.

Some have taught that God is the world-soul, while others that he is the formal principle of all things–this is supposed to have been the theory of the followers of Amaury de Bènes; others, most foolishly, taught that he is primary matter.[1] All make the same mistake of thinking that in some way God can enter into composition with other things. He is the first efficient cause, and an efficient cause is not numerically identical with its effect. He is the essential efficient cause, immediately and directly active. This cannot be said of any part of a composite, where the whole thing is the active cause; to speak with accuracy, it is not the hand that acts, but the man through his hand. God is the first thing absolutely speaking, and no part of a whole can be that.

❧ Though God is wholly simple we must still address him with a multitude of names. Our mind is not able to grasp his essence. We have to start from the things about us, which have diverse perfections though their root and origin in God is one. Because we cannot name objects except in the way we understand them, for words are the signs of concepts, we can name God only from the terms employed elsewhere. These are manifold, therefore we must make use of many terms. Were we to see God in himself we would not call on a multitude of words; our knowledge would be as simple as his nature is simple. We look forward to this in the day of our glory; *in that day there shall be one Lord and his name one* (Zach. xiv. 9).

❧ Though our lips can only stammer, says Gregory, we yet must sing the high things of God. What is not made cannot be called perfect in the original sense of the word.[2] Yet because we speak of perfection in connexion with things which are achieved from potentiality, the term can be extended to mean whatever is not wanting in actual being, whether produced or not.

❧ When God is called universally perfect because no kind of perfec-

[1] Amaury de Bènes (d. 1206–7) and his contemporary David de Dinant (or Dinan), who were condemned together during the period of the first official reactions to the revival of Aristotle. Thèry suggests that St. Thomas's unwonted fling was in order to show that the cause of true Aristoteleanism was not compromised by the censures: it is possible that the term *folly* is not so much a piece of invective as a conventional expression for what was untutored and silly in the archaic sense.

[2] *Perfectus*, from *perficio*, *facio*, to make.

tion is wanting in him, the statement can be supported on two counts. First, everything brought to perfection pre-exists in the producing cause in a more excellent mode. Dionysius touches this when he declares that God is not this or that, but is all as the cause of all. Secondly, God is pure existence subsisting essentially and consequently contains within himself the whole perfection of existence: all perfections are embraced in the perfection of existence, and therefore no single perfection is lacking in God. Dionysius also refers to this in maintaining that God does not exist in any special manner, but holds beforehand within himself all being, absolutely, boundlessly, uniformly.

☙ All things desire God himself in desiring their own proper perfections, inasmuch as these are so many likenesses of him. Some know him for himself, and this is proper to rational creatures; others know some share of his goodness as stretching into the life of the senses; others have purely natural and unconscious appetites for him, because they are directed to their ends by a higher intelligence.

☙ Divine goodness neither depends on, nor can gain from, the goodness of the universe. The perfection of the universe is necessarily committed to the particular goods of its essential components, and its well-being is supplemented by factors of safety and adornment. The idea behind divine volition may be sometimes of what is fitting, sometimes of what is useful, sometimes of what is hypothetically necessary on the supposition that the present scheme of things should work. But absolute necessity is present only when God wills himself.

☙ Goodness is an analogical idea, divided into the honourable, the delightful, and the useful, and not predicated of them equally, but according to that order of priority. The division is rather of contrasted notions than of different things. Those goods are honourable and of true worth which are dear in themselves. Those things are delightful that give us pleasure, though sometimes they may be harmful or unworthy. Utilities have no attraction in themselves, but are desired, rather like bitter medicine, as leading to something else.

❦ Boundlessness does not exclude plurality, except in so far as it rules out determinateness, which is the first principle of plurality. There are two kinds of determinateness, namely of limitation and of distinction. In the divine nature there is no kind of limitation, but there is distinctiveness, and in two ways: first, as being distinguished by essence from creatures, as the unlimited from the limited; second, according to the distinction of persons by the relation of origin, which distinction is because of the contrast in relations, not because of limitation.

❦ God is everywhere and in every place, first because he is in all things giving them substance, power, and operation. Since place is real he is present there. Also things are in place because they fill it, and God fills every place, but not as a body, for so one occupant excludes another, whereas he displaces nothing.

❦ Spiritual things are in place, not like bodies by the contact of dimensive quantity, but by the contact of power.

❦ In two senses creatures are said to be in God. First, in so far as they are contained and preserved by the divine power, even as we say that things within our power are in us. So by their own very reality are creatures in God. This is the meaning of the Apostle's words; *in him we live and move and have our being* (Acts xvii. 28). Secondly, things are said to be in God as in the one who knows them, in which sense they are in God by their especial meanings, which in God are none other than the divine essence. Things in God are the divine nature. And because the divine essence is life, though without a process of coming to be and dying away, we can say in this context that things are living and deathless in God.

❦ Nothing wanes or waxes in God, for he is unchangeable and his being is entire all at once.

❦ As we have to penetrate composite things in order to reach simple things, so we must go through time to come to the knowledge of eternity. In successive changes where one part follows another we apprehend time by numbering the before and after in movement. There is no before and after to be reckoned in constant and changeless reality. The form of eternity lies in the apprehension of that uniformity. Furthermore those things are measured by time which have a temporal beginning and end; what is wholly invariable and without succession has neither beginning nor end. So therefore eternity is signified by these two clauses: first, that a thing in eternity can be closed neither prospectively nor retrospectively; secondly, that it is entire all at once without any successiveness.

❦ The apprehension of time is caused by the perception of the changing instant, the apprehension of eternity by that of the enduring instant.

❦ The *now* of time is not time, the *now* of eternity is really the same as eternity.

❦ In appreciating what happens in time, we should remark that a mind bound up in it is differently placed from a mind entirely outside its series. When many are travelling the same road, each of the company knows those ahead and those behind; he sees his immediate companion, he has seen those who have gone ahead, but those well behind he cannot see. But he who is no part of the throng but watches from high above is in a position to take in the whole convoy. He is able to see simultaneously all who are on the march, not as met before and after, but as all together in their order.

Because our knowledge is enclosed in the order of time, either directly or indirectly, the time-factor enters into our calculations, and our knowledge reckons things as past, present, or future. Past, in memory; present, in experience; future, by anticipation in present causes. Future events are either certainties, when they are wholly predetermined in their causes, or conjectures, when they can usually be forecast, or unknown, when their causes are not yet committed to action.

God, however, is entirely above the order of time. He is at the peak of eternity, surmounting everything all at once. Thence the stream of time can be seen in one simple glance.

❧ Eternity is compared to time as an indivisible to a continuous stretch. There is diversity of parts in time according to a before and after of successive events, as in a line there are points in different places yet related to one another. Eternity, however, has no before and after, and is simultaneously entire.

❧ Though in himself supremely knowable, God surpasses the power of a limited intelligence by very excess of truth. The bat blinks in the blaze of the sun. Impressed by this thought, some have concluded that no created intellect can see the nature of God.

But it is an awkward conclusion. For since man's ultimate happiness consists in his highest activity, were he never able to see God, then either he could never reach his bliss or this would lie in something other than God, which is alien to Christian belief. Moreover, it is philosophically unsound, for there is an inborn desire of knowing cause when effect is seen – this is the spring of wonder. If, therefore, the mind of rational creatures could never see the first cause of things this natural desire would be pointless.

❧ But through no created likeness can the nature of God be seen.

❧ What is seen in imaginative visions is not God's nature, but images which represent him after a fashion, as do the metaphorical figures in holy writ.

❧ By native power no created mind can see the essence of God. Knowledge implies the presence of the known in the knower in the knower's own way. To know subsisting being is natural to the divine mind alone. It is above the natural ability of created mind. Therefore a created mind cannot see the divine essence except God by his grace shows and gives himself.

❧ The divine essence is being itself. As other intelligible forms, which are not their own very being, are united to the mind through a mental likeness whereby they inform and make actual the intellect, so the divine essence can be united to created intellect as that which is both actually understood and of itself making the intellect actual.

❧ Our natural knowledge begins with sensation, and therefore can be led as far as sensible things can take us. Through these effects, which do not equal the virtue of their cause, we cannot know the full power of God or, consequently, see his essence. Nevertheless they are his effects and dependent on their cause. We can be led by them so far as to know of his existence and some necessary attributes. He is the first universal cause surpassing all his effects, and we can know his relationship to creatures and their difference from him.

❧ This name, *He Who Is*, is the most proper name for God, and for three reasons. First, for denotation; it does not signify a kind of form, but being itself. Second, for universality; it determines no mode of being, but names the boundless sea of substance. Third, for connotation; it intimates being entirely present, free of past and future.

❧ Hold steadily to the truth that God has most assured knowledge of all things knowable at any time and by any mind: it cannot be otherwise.

His being is identical with his understanding. As his substance is pure existence so also is it pure understanding. Here nothing is lacking that can relate to knowledge, for every hint of knowledge is held in the sheer form of knowledge. Since his being is one, simple, firm, and enduring, it follows that by one single insight God enjoys eternal and unwavering knowledge of everything.

Indeed in the first cause things exist more nobly even than they do in themselves, for what exists in another exists according to the mode of that one's substance, and the substance of God is his understanding. Everything that is in any way real, therefore, exists intelligibly in God at the height of his substance, and is there known completely.

Were the godhead unconscious it would be like a man who slumbers and worthy of no great reverence.

❧ In God knowledge is consummate – this grows on us when we reflect that unconscious things have no other form but their own, whereas conscious things have a natural capacity to possess the forms of other things as well. That is the root difference between them. Unconscious nature is more restricted and limited, while conscious nature has a greater breadth and reach. Aristotle had this in mind when he spoke of the soul as being somehow all things.

Now the restriction of form comes from matter, and therefore the less material a form the ampler it is. The non-materiality of a thing is the reason why it can know, and the mode of its non-materiality sets the measure of its knowledge. Plants are unable to know because they are earthbound, but sense is cognitive for it receives non-material impressions, while the mind is freer still and less involved in matter. Since God is at the summit of non-materiality he is at the summit of knowledge.

❧ Let us make quite clear that there is no discursiveness in divine knowledge. In our knowledge there is a double process; one of succession only, when from actually understanding one object we turn our attention to another; the other of causality, as when we arrive at conclusions through principles. The first process cannot apply to God, for the multiple objects we understand successively when they are taken in themselves can be understood all at once when they are seen in one principle. God sees everything in one, namely, in himself alone. Nor does the second process apply; first, because it entails succession, for in working from principles to conclusions we do not simultaneously consider them both; secondly, because it is a process from the known to the unknown.

❧ He knows himself perfectly. To know a thing its power must be gauged perfectly, which involves the knowledge of all things to which its power can extend.

❧ Lest anyone should fancy that God stands utterly aloof and apart from everything, that on our part he is beyond our ken, while he for his part does not cherish what is below him, Dionysius adds that divine knowledge is circum-apprehensive of all things because it knows all properties and circumstances, and comprehensive because it perfectly knows all natures, and pre-apprehensive because it does not acquire knowledge from things but as their cause forestalls them.

❧ Some would withhold the knowledge of singular facts[1] from the perfection of the divine mind and they would maintain their position along seven lines of reasoning.

First, from the very condition of singularity. It is alleged that no spiritual power can know determinate matter which is the principle of singularity, for knowledge results from an assimilation of knower and known; whence in our case only those powers using material organs can apprehend singulars. The pure intellect cannot know them because it is spiritual, much less therefore can the divine intellect, which more than any other is far away from matter.

Second, singulars are not eternal. Either they are always known by God or they are known at one time and not known at another. The former alternative is ruled out because there is no true science of what is not, science being about true things, and non-existents are not true things. The latter alternative is ruled out because divine knowledge is altogether invariable.

Third, some singulars happen contingently and are not produced of necessity. They can be objects of certitude only after they have actually happened. Certitude is infallible, whereas the anticipation of a contingent event is fallible; if the opposite could not come about the event would be already necessary. We can enjoy no certitude about a future contingency, though we may hazard a shrewd guess. But all divine knowledge must be supposed to be most certain and infallible.

Fourth, some of these singular effects are caused by will. Now before it has taken place an event can be known solely in its cause. But the motion of will can be known with certitude by him alone in whose power the decision lies. Therefore God cannot have certain foreknowledge of singular events that depend on what we are freely going to do.

Fifth, an argument from the very infinity of singulars. The infinite, that is the indefinite, is unknowable as such, for everything known is measured by mind; on this account art scorns shapelessness. Singulars,

[1] Real individuals, such as *Justinian*; not merely particularized generalities, such as *an emperor*.

however, are infinite, at least potentially. Therefore it seems impossible that God should know them.

Sixth, from the paltriness of singulars. Since the nobility of a science is pitched according to the dignity of its object, so the triviality of an object redounds on the corresponding knowledge. The divine mind, however, is of all the most elevated and the least tolerant of pettiness.

Seventh, from the wickedness present in some singular events. Since the known is somehow in the knower and evil cannot exist in God, it seems to follow that God simply does not know the evil and deprivation appropriate to imperfect minds.

Let us sift these arguments so that we may throw away what is contrary to the truth and show forth the perfection of divine knowledge. We shall show, first, that the divine mind knows singulars; second, and things not yet actual; third, and future contingencies with infallible knowledge; fourth, and the motions of the will; fifth, and infinites; sixth, and the humblest and vilest things; seventh, and all evils, deprivations, and defects.[1]

☙ To know things properly means knowing them, not merely in the mass, but also in their distinctiveness from one another. So does God know things, *piercing even to the dividing asunder of soul and spirit, and of the joints and marrow, a discerner of the thoughts and intents of the heart, neither is there any creature that is not manifest in his sight* (Hebr. iv. 12).

Some have slipped into the mistake of thinking that God knows things in general because everything shares in the common nature of being, and that by knowing himself as the fount of being, he knows the nature of being and all things in so far as they belong to being.[2] But this will not do, for to know something in general and not in its peculiarities is to know it imperfectly. Our mind, bringing out what is latent to begin with and going on to develop its full activity, starts with universal and confused knowledge before reaching to proper understanding.

We should say, then, that God knows things other than himself, not only inasmuch as they share in the general nature of reality, but also

[1] Not all of these assumptions are dealt with in the passages cited here.

[2] An opinion attributed to Averroes.

according to their special characteristics. Some have attempted to illustrate how God can understand many things in one knowledge by the example of a conscious centre that would know all radii, or a conscious light that would know all colours. But such examples, though well enough as illustrations of universal causality, fail here because multiple and diverse things derive from such a unitary principle in what they share in common, not in what makes them peculiar; and so by it they would be known in general, not in detail.

In God it is otherwise. Whatsoever is of value in any creature pre-exists in God; all perfections are all together and contained in him superbly, not only for what they have in common, namely being, but also for their special notes of difference. Every kind of form is a perfection. So all are anticipated in God, not merely where they agree with one another, but also where they are exclusively themselves. Consequently God, who contains all perfections, should not be compared to created natures as common to proper, nor as unity to number, nor as centre to radii, but as perfect actuality to imperfect actualities.

It is clear that imperfect realizations can be known by a perfect actuality with distinctness, not merely in a sweeping generalization. The essence of God contains whatever is of value in other things, and much more besides, and so God can know things other than himself with proper knowledge. The proper nature of each consists in this, that in some degree it participates in the divine perfection. God would not know himself perfectly did he not also know how his perfections could be shared; neither would he perfectly know the very nature of being unless he knew all the variations on being.

☙ God knows all things that are real in any way whatsoever. Things that are not real absolutely may be real relatively. Things are real absolutely when they are actual and exist. Things that are not actual may be in the power of God or in the power of the creature, whether in active power or passive potentiality, whether in the ability of thought or imagination to invest an object with any sort of meaning or interest. Whatever they are and however they can come about or be thought of or alluded to, all are known by God, though actually they do not exist.

Yet some difference should be noted among the things that are not actual. Though some of them are not actual now, nevertheless they have been or will be actual, and all these are said to be known by the knowledge of vision. For since God's act of understanding, which is his being, is measured by eternity, which is without succession and comprehends all time, the instantaneous glance of God falls on all things in any period of time as on things present to him. But there are other things in the power of God or the creature which are not, nor have been, nor ever will be; these he is said to know by the knowledge of simple intelligence, not of vision, for vision implies a real object apart from the viewer.

❧ By his art an artist may know even those things he has not yet wrought. The forms of art flow from his knowledge into external material there to constitute works of art. There is nothing to prevent his entertaining thoughts about forms that have not yet outwardly appeared.

❧ The divine essence contains all real nobilities by transcending rather than by combining them all. Every form, peculiar and generic alike, is a perfection, for it accentuates reality, and betrays imperfection only when it falls short of authentic reality. The divine mind, therefore, in its own essence can comprehend what is innermostly peculiar to all things, understanding where they succeed and where they fail in rendering divine perfection. So the divine essence, itself sheerly perfect, can be taken as the proper reason of singular things. Now because the special character of one thing is distinct from the special character of another, we can attribute to the divine mind a distinction and plurality as regards the objects understood, for within the divine mind is the proper reason of each and all. This is because God understands the proper relation of similarity which they bear to him. In consequence the reasons of things in the divine mind are many and distinct just because God knows how things are assimilable to him in many and diverse ways. Augustine speaks about God making a man by one reason and a horse by another; he says also that the reasons of things are many in the divine mind. This in some measure safeguards the opinion of Plato, who postulated ideas according to which are formed all things existing in matter.

I

❦ The first man did not see God in his essence as a matter of course in his original state of life; though perhaps you could say that he saw him so in rapture, when God *cast a deep sleep upon Adam*, as it says in *Genesis* (ii. 21). And the reason is that since the divine essence simply is bliss itself, the mind of someone who sees the divine essence has the same attitude towards God as anyone does towards bliss in general. Now it is obvious that no one can wilfully and deliberately turn away from bliss as such; for man naturally and necessarily wants bliss and shuns unhappiness. Thus nobody who sees God in his essence can wilfully and deliberately turn away from God, which is what sin is. And for this reason all who see God in his essence are so solidly established in the love of God that never can they sin. Since then Adam did sin, it is obvious that he never used to see God in his essence.

However, he did know God with a loftier sort of knowledge than we do now; and thus his knowledge was somehow or other half way between knowledge in our present state and knowledge in the home-country, where God is seen in his essence. To see why, we should consider that the sight of God in his essence is distinguished from the sight of God in his creatures. Now the loftier a creature is, and the more it resembles God, the clearer is the sight of God to be obtained through it; just as a man is seen more perfectly in a mirror the more distinctly his image is reflected in it. Thus it is clear that God is seen with much more distinction in his intelligible effects than in sensible and bodily ones.[1]

But a full and lucid consideration of God's intelligible effects is made practically impossible for man in his present state by the sensible ones which distract and engross his attention. And yet, as it says in *Ecclesiastes* (vii. 30), *God made man right.* And this rightness of man as he was divinely established at the beginning consisted in the lower parts of his nature being subject to the higher, and the higher not being hampered by the lower. And so the first man used not to be hampered by external things from the clear and steady contemplation of God's intelligible effects, which he would observe, whether by natural or gratuitous knowledge, under the illumination of the first truth. And thus Augustine says: *Perhaps God used of old to speak to the first man as he now speaks with angels, illuminating their minds with unchangeable truth itself,*[2] . . . *even though they did not have such a grasp of the divine essence as the angels do.* So therefore by such intelligible effects of God he used to know God more luminously than we could do now.

Hence: 1. Man had bliss in Paradise, but not that perfect bliss into which he was to have been translated, and which consists in beholding the divine essence. However, he did enjoy *the life of bliss after a certain fashion*, as Augustine says, in so far as he had a certain natural entirety and perfection.

2. A good will is an orderly will. But the first man would not have had an orderly will if in the state of meriting he had wanted to have what was promised him as a reward – wages without work.

3. There are two sorts of intermediary; one in which the thing said to be seen through the intermediary is itself seen simultaneously, as when a man is seen in a mirror and is seen simultaneously with the mirror;[3]

[1] By intelligible effects and sensible effects he can scarcely mean distinct and separate items in the created universe; it is rather a case of the same created object being on the one hand manifest to the senses, and on the other manifest in their order and meaning to the mind.

[2] For Augustine the unchangeable truth itself is simply God himself, as shedding the light of intelligibility over all his creation; the light that enlightens every man who comes into the world.

[3] He does not mean when you see the man directly and at the same time in the mirror out of the corner of your eye, for in this case your seeing him in the mirror is not a means to your seeing the man, whom you are also seeing apart from his reflection in the mirror. He

the other is the intermediary by knowledge of which we come across something we had not known, and such is the intermediary or middle term of logical demonstration. And God used to be seen, I agree, without that sort of intermediary, but not without the first sort. For the first man did not have to arrive at knowledge of God by demonstration proceeding from some effect to God as cause, as we have to do; but in his own way he knew God simultaneously in his effects, especially the intelligible ones.

Likewise it is worth observing that the obscurity implied by the word 'riddle' can be taken in two ways. On the one hand, any created thing you like can be regarded as something obscure and dim compared with the immensity of the divine brightness; and in this sense Adam used to see God in riddles because he saw him in created effects. On the other hand, you can take obscurity as a consequence of sin, which hampers man in his observation of intelligible things by engrossing him in sensible ones; and in this sense he did not see God in a riddle.

II

❦ Some of the ancient Doctors of the Church were led by consideration of the lust which besmirches copulation in the present state to suppose that in the state of innocence there would have been no procreation by copulation. So Gregory of Nyssa for one says that in Paradise the human race would have been multiplied by other means, just as then angels were multiplied without mating, by an operation of divine power. And he says that God made male and female before they sinned with his eye on the manner of procreation which would be used after they sinned, of which he had foreknowledge.

But this is not a reasonable position. For everything that is natural to man is neither withdrawn from nor given to him by sin. Now it is plain that it is natural to man in his animal life, which he had even before sin, as we have seen, to procreate by copulation, as it is to the other perfect

---

means when you see his reflection in the mirror and are thereby made simultaneously aware of the man himself, through his reflection indeed, but without any discursive process of reasoning *from* his reflection.

animals.[1] And this is indicated by the organs assigned by nature to this function. And therefore it cannot be said of these natural organs, any more than of the other organs, that they would not have been used before sin.

There are two factors, then, in copulation in the present state that must be considered. One is the fact of nature, namely the mating of male and female for procreation. For in every kind of generation there is required an active and a passive capacity. Since then in all living things that show a distinction of sex the active capacity is in the male and the passive in the female, the rhythm of nature demands that male and female should mate in copulation for procreating.

But the other thing that can be considered in copulation is the extravagance of desire which disfigures it. This would not have been found in the state of innocence, in which the lower energies were completely subject to the reason. So Augustine says: *God forbid that we should suppose progeny could not have been sown without the disease of lust. But those organs would have been moved at the bidding of the will just like the others now, without passion or the prickings of allurement, in tranquillity of mind and body.*

Hence: 1. In Paradise man would have been like an angel in his spiritual mind, while still having an animal life in the body. But after the resurrection man will be like an angel, having been rendered spiritual both in soul and in body. So the cases are not similar.

2. As Augustine says, the reason our first parents did not mate in Paradise was that once the woman was fashioned they were in next to no time thrown out of Paradise for sin; or else they were waiting for the definite time of mating to be laid down by the same divine authority which had given them the general commandment to be fruitful.

3. Animals lack reason. So what makes man like the animals in copulation is the inability of reason to temper the pleasure of copulation and the heat of desire. But in the state of innocence there would have been nothing of this sort that was not tempered by reason. Not that the pleasurable sensation would have been any the less intense, as some say,

[1] The perfect animals, in Aristotle's terminology, are those which are endowed with all five senses, as against the imperfect ones which may have only the one sense of touch, like limpets.

for the pleasure of sense would have been all the greater, given the greater purity of man's nature and sensibility of his body. But the pleasure urge would not have squandered itself in so disorderly a fashion on this sort of pleasure when it was ruled by reason. It is not demanded by this empire of reason that the pleasurable sensation should be any the less, but that the pleasure urge should not clutch at the pleasure in an immoderate fashion; and by 'immoderate' I mean going beyond the measure of reason. Thus a sober man has no less pleasure in food taken moderately than a greedy man; but his pleasure urge does not wallow so much in this sort of pleasure. And this is the bearing of Augustine's words, which do not exclude intensity of pleasure from the state of innocence, but impetuous lust and disturbance of mind.

And so in the state of innocence no particular esteem would have attached to continence, which is not esteemed in this present time for its lack of fruitfulness, but for its freedom from disordered lust. But in that time there would have been fruitfulness without lust.

4. As Augustine says, in that state *the husband would shed himself in the lap of his wife*[1] *without any damage to integrity. . . . For the man's seed could have been introduced into the womb of his consort and the integrity of the female genital organ have been preserved, just as now the same integrity can be preserved and the flow of menstrual blood released from the womb of a virgin. . . . For just as the bowels of the woman would have been expanded for giving birth by impulse of maturation and not by any pangs of travail, so for conceiving no lustful appetite but a rational choice of will would have joined both natures together.*

III

Let us suppose, in agreement with Catholic belief and against some people's mistaken views, that in fact the world has not existed from eternity, but once had a beginning, as holy writ testifies. The doubt emerges, nevertheless, whether it could always have existed.[2]

[1] There is a literary allusion in this phrase to the *Aeneid* viii. 407.

[2] This *opusculum de Aeternitate Mundi* is, together with the *de Ente et Essentia* and the *de Unitate Intellectus*, the most celebrated of St. Thomas's smaller works, and is here quoted extensively as a typical example of his mode of arguing by methodic exclusion.

In order to open out the truth of the matter let us begin by observing where we agree with our opponents and where we differ. If crediting eternity to something other than God is equivalent to meaning that it was not made by him, that would be an ungracious error, not against faith merely, but also against the doctrine of philosophers, who teach and prove that anything existing in any way whatsoever cannot exist unless caused by the greatest and truest being. If all that is meant, however, is that a thing always was, though caused by God in its entirety, then we are on the point of the debate.

Were this called impossible the reason alleged would be, either that God could not make something that always was, or that it could not be done even when allowances have been made for omnipotence. Both sides agree on the first proposition that God can do everything. What has to be looked into is the second proposition.

That it cannot be done will be supported on one of two grounds; either because such a reality would exclude passive potentiality, or because it would involve a contradiction in terms.

As to the first, let it be remembered that no process of becoming precedes the established being of a pure spirit; there is no passive potentiality before its existence, and no production of it from presupposed material. Nevertheless, God can produce a pure spirit in existence, and has done so. In this context it may be admitted that a thing caused by God could not exist always if this implied an eternally pre-existing passive principle. However, this is not entailed in the statement that God could make a reality that always was.

As to the second, we speak of an impossibility on account of the inherent repugnance of the ideas involved, for instance that contradictories should be simultaneously true. Though some hold that God can do the impossible, while others deny it because of the nonentity of the impossible, in truth it is out of the question for God to produce what would be a self-destructive object. Yet to affirm that God could do it would not be contrary to faith, though I hold that it would be false. For instance, to assert that what has happened has not happened is a contradiction in terms, and similarly that omnipotence may cause things that have happened to be as if they had not happened at all; whoever says this, remarks Augustine, does not notice that what he is saying is that some things are true inasmuch as they are false. All the same some authorities have devoutly professed that God can so wipe out the past, nor were they deemed heretical.

Therefore we should look closely to see whether these two notes, namely *caused by God* and *always existing*, are incompatible. Whatever the merits of the case the charge of heresy cannot enter here, though, were the ideas mutually exclusive, I hold that an everlasting creature would be a figment. But if the ideas do not clash it would be otherwise, and to deny its possibility would be a mistake. Furthermore, it would derogate from omnipotence, which exceeds our power and understanding, to say that we could conceive of something God could not produce. Nor is sin at all relevant, for that as such is emptiness. The whole question, therefore, boils down to this: Are the ideas *entirely creaturely* and *without a beginning in duration* mutually exclusive or not?

That they do not cancel out may be shown as follows. Their mutual exclusiveness could only be on account of one or both of the following postulates; first, that a cause must precede its effect in duration; secondly, that non-being must precede being in duration, as when we say that creation is from nothing.

Observe that there is no need for the efficient cause, in this case God, to precede his effects in duration, unless he so wills it. To start with, no cause instantaneously producing effects necessarily antedates them in duration, and God is a cause able to produce effects suddenly and not through a process of change. The major premiss may be made clearer by induction from sudden effects such as radiations and so forth, and may be proved by deduction as follows: when a thing is supposed to exist, at that very moment the beginning of its action can also be supposed, as appears even with things that come to be through natural processes, for at the very instant that fire begins so does heating. Now in an instantaneous action the beginning and the end are simultaneous, indeed identical. At the very instant an efficient cause is conceived of as producing its instantaneous effect, the term of its action is also posited. The action and the finish are instantaneous. Well then, it is not contradictory to conceive of a cause producing an instantaneous effect and not preceding it in duration. This of course would be inconceivable in the case of a cause producing its effects through successive stages; here the beginning must precede the finish. Because people usually deal with causality working through a process, they do not readily recognize that an efficient cause is not necessarily antecedent to its effect in duration – laying down the law on special problems is rather apt to go along with lack of experience.

It cannot be objected against this line of reasoning that God acts through his will, for the will does not necessarily precede its effects in duration, except when its action is deliberative, and far be it from us to attribute deliberation to God.[1]

Furthermore, a cause producing the whole substance of an effect is no less potent than is a cause producing the form, indeed, it is much more potent, for it does not merely educe a form from potential material. Yet a transforming cause may so act that whenever it exists its effects exist also, as with the light of the sun. With much stronger reason can God so act that his effect is whenever he is.

Then again, a cause that could not produce a contemporary effect would be lacking its complement, for a complete cause and its effect are simultaneous. But nothing is lacking in God. Therefore his effects may always be, on the supposition that he always is, and he is not bound to precede them in duration.

Lastly, the will of the willer does not diminish his power, least of all with God. The opponents of the Aristotelian argument – to the effect that creatures have always existed because like always makes like – urge that this is tantamount to treating God as a non-voluntary cause. But the same objection applies to what they would admit, namely that he is a voluntary cause but cannot unmake the things he has caused so as to make them as though they had never been.

Hence, to say that an efficient cause need not antedate its effect manifestly offers no violence to the mind. It now remains to inquire whether on account of its being made out of nothing it is impossible to conceive of a creature that never was not.

In the *Monologion* Anselm shows that this is not a contradiction: the third interpretation, he says, of the words *made out of nothing* is when we understand that it is made, but that there is not anything out of

[1] God does not calculate, or make up his mind in stages, as we do.

which it is made. A similar turn of speech is employed when somebody grieving without cause is said to grieve about nothing. According to this construction no awkwardness follows if we mean that all beings, apart from the supreme being, are made out of nothing, that is, not made out of anything. Nor is precedence implied, such as would mean that once there was nothing, and then afterwards there was something.

Even were precedence indicated, and the statement to bear the sense that the creature was made after nothing, this term *after* would mean precedence only in the most general sense. For precedence may be of nature or of duration. The general and universal does not imply the particular and proper.[1] That the creature is after nothingness does not imply that once in duration there was nothing and then afterwards something was, but merely that nothing is prior by nature to reality. For that which a thing has of itself is prior to what it receives from another; now a creature's reality is received from another; therefore left to itself and considered in itself it is as nothing, and there is nothing in it before being.

Nor would it follow that non-being and being would be simultaneous unless nothing precedes being. For we do not say that if creatures always were there would be a time when there was nothing, but that creaturely beings are such that they would be non-beings were they left to themselves.

Clearly, then, there is no contradiction in affirming that a thing is created and also that it never was non-existent. It is certainly strange that Augustine did not notice any, for it would have been a decisive disproof of the eternity of the world, which he attacked on many scores but not on that. On the contrary, he rather hints that no contradiction is present.

There are other objections which I skip for the present, partly because they are dealt with elsewhere and partly because their very weakness lends force to the position they oppose.

[1] That is, the general category of precedence, in things' natures, does not entail the sub-category of precedence in duration.

THE INCARNATION

❧ In proclaiming the undivided Christ some heretics went to the length of saying that God and man were not just one single person, but one nature as well. The error started from Arius. From those texts of Holy Scripture which refer to Christ – meaning his human nature – being less than the Father, he concluded that Christ's animating principle was solely the Word of God. This took the place of soul in his body. And when he said, *my Father is greater than I* (John xiv. 28), and when we read that he prayed or grew sad, these words, deeds, and sufferings were attributed by the Arians to the nature of the Son of God. The conclusion was pushed, and the union of God with man explained as being in nature as well as in person, since body and soul constitute the unity of human nature.

The underlying mistake concerned the mystery of the Trinity, and is corrected by professing that Father and Son are equal. Concerning the Incarnation, the doctrine that the Word was the substitute for a human soul can be disproved in several ways.

Soul is united to body as substantial form of body. God cannot be the substantial form of anything. If perhaps you urge that Arius would have granted this where the supreme God, the Father, was in question, then it should be pointed out that the same is also true of angels, which by nature cannot be united to bodies as forms, since essentially they are completely spiritual. Much less, then, can the Son of God, through whom, as Arius professed, the angels were made, enter into such union.

Moreover, we deny what Arius falsely declared, that the Son of God is a creature. All spiritual creatures reach their happiness through him, and now such is their joy that sorrow cannot touch them. Much less, therefore, can God the Son grieve in his nature, or fear. Yet we read, *he began to fear and be heavy* (Mark xiv. 33), and he told his sorrow, *my soul is sorrowful unto death* (Mark xiv. 34). Sadness is not just a bodily reaction; it is experienced by a conscious substance. Together with the Word and the flesh, there was a substantial reality in Christ which could feel sadness, and this we call the soul.

Again, if Christ assumed what was ours in order to cleanse us from sin, and since it is more necessary for our souls to be cleansed than our bodies – for the soul is the source and subject of sin – he took soul, the predominant part of us, with body, not body without soul.

❧ Apollinaris began by agreeing with Arius in holding that there was no other soul in Christ save the Word of God. Since, however, he did not subscribe to the doctrine of Arius that the Son of God was a creature, and since he recognized that many traits of Christ are proper neither to the Creator nor to the human body alone, he was compelled, though still thinking that the Word took the place of reason and intelligence, to postulate a soul, non-rational and non-intellectual, which sensitively quickened the body and was the seat of emotion.

This doctrine strikes alike at the genuineness of human nature and at the purpose of the Incarnation. It means that the form of Christ's human body was not a rational soul, whereas nothing queer or unnatural should be imagined about the Incarnation. Moreover, the restoration of human nature is principally an affair of its intellectual part. That is where sin begins, and that, therefore, should be taken over by God. Furthermore, we read that Christ marvelled. Now admiring is an act of the rational soul, and is quite impossible to God. Christ's sadness leads us to infer the presence of a sensitive soul, his wonder the presence of an intelligent soul.

❧ Eutyches went some of the way with Arius and Apollinaris. True, he did not deny a human soul or mind to Christ, nor any integral part of human nature. All the same he postulated one nature for both God and man after the Incarnation.

That his opinion was mistaken appears on several counts. The divine nature, complete and beyond all change, cannot enter into the make-up of another nature. One kind of thing unites with another either by being absorbed, like food into living tissue, or by consuming it, as fire destroys wood, or by the transmutation of both into a third thing, as when elements make a compound. The immutability of the divine nature forbids its entering into any of these three processes.

Again, when we view the scale of reality, we notice that the addition to a subject of a greater perfection changes its type: thus an animate thing is different in kind from an inanimate thing, a sensitive thing from an animate thing, an intelligent sensitive thing from a merely sensitive animate thing. Had the one nature Eutyches credited to Christ possessed essentially divine characteristics in addition to the human it would have been specifically different from human nature. He would not have been a man true to human type, whereas the Gospel declares he was born according to the flesh: *the book of the generation of Jesus Christ, the son of David, the son of Abraham* (Matt. i. 1).

❧ Photinus lessened the mystery of the Incarnation by denying Christ's divine nature: the Manichees did the same by denying his human nature. Fancying all bodily nature to be caused by the power of evil, and thinking how unfitting it would have been for the Son of God to assume a creature of the devil, they therefore laid it down that Christ had flesh only in appearance, not in reality, and that the Gospel narratives about his humanity are pieces of imagination, not accounts of physical fact.

They contradict the express statements of Holy Writ, that Christ was born of a virgin, that he was circumcised, was hungry, ate food, and performed the functions appropriate to human nature. Were the Manichees right, then the Gospel narrative would be wrong. Christ said of himself: *To this end was I born, and for this cause came I into the world, that I should bear witness to the truth* (John xviii. 37). He would instead have attested a falsehood, especially as he foretold sufferings that would have been unreal had he lacked true flesh, for he foretold that he would be betrayed into men's hands, and that they would spit on him, scourge him, crucify him. To say that he was merely acting a part would be to load him with a lie.

To shake a true conviction is the work of a deceiver. Christ set himself to remove from men's minds any idea that he was a phantom. When he appeared to his disciples and they thought they saw a spirit or ghost he said, *Handle me, and see, for a spirit hath not flesh and bones, as you see me to have* (Luke xxiv. 39). Before that, when they were troubled as he came walking to them on the waves and fancied they saw an apparition, *Have a good heart*, he said, *it is I, fear ye not* (Mark vi. 51).

❧ Though he acknowledged that Christ possessed a truly human body, Valentinus nevertheless taught that Christ's flesh was not taken from the Virgin, but that a body was transmitted from heaven through her, without taking anything from her. It was as though water ran along a conduit. But this gainsays Bible truth: *Jesus Christ our Lord was made of the seed of David according to the flesh* (Rom. i. 3). And again, *God sent forth his Son, made of a woman* (Gal. iv. 4). And again, *Jacob begat Joseph the husband of Mary, of whom was born Jesus, who is called Christ* (Matt. i. 16). And Mary is called *his mother* (Matt. i. 18). These statements would not be true had he possessed a heavenly kind of body, not born of the Virgin. When St. Paul says, *The first man is of the earth, earthy; the second man is the Lord from heaven* (1 Cor. xv. 47), he means that Christ's divinity, not his bodily substance, descended from heaven. Why should a heavenly body enter the Virgin's womb if nothing was to be taken from her? The history would have been fiction, the process a mock-birth. All deceit is alien to Christ. We should confess quite bluntly, that Christ came forth from the Virgin's womb having been formed from her body.

❧ The Catholic Faith professes that Christ's body is of the same kind as ours, and with this body goes a true rational soul, and simultaneously the perfect Deity, all three substantial and together in one person, not in one nature.

Some writers have gone astray when expounding this truth. Observing that whatever comes to an already substantially complete subject is then joined to it in accidental union – thus a man and the clothes he wears are not combined in substantial union, for they do not make up one substance – they concluded that Christ's humanity was connected to the Divinity in the person of the Son like a vesture put on; they adduced St. Paul's words in support, *in habit found as a man* (Phil. ii. 7). Again, observing that an individual of rational nature, in other words, a person, results from the union of soul and body, they concluded that from the direct union of Christ's soul with his body a human personality could not fail to result. Consequently there were two persons in Christ, the person assuming and the person assumed, as there would be in a man clothed were his garments a person.

To avoid such a conclusion others postulated that Christ's soul was never directly united to his body, but that the person of the Son separately assumed soul and body. Striving to avoid one difficulty they landed themselves in a greater. One unavoidable consequence of this doctrine would be that Christ was not a genuine man, for human nature is a composite of soul and body. Another consequence: he would be without true flesh and true bodily members, for eye is not truly human apart from soul, nor is hand, nor flesh and bone: they would be human only in a manner of speaking, as in a picture or statue. Another consequence: Christ would not really have died, for death is the deprivation of life, and cannot happen either to the Divinity or to a body which had never been alive. Another consequence: Christ would not have felt, for body does not feel unless quickened by soul.

❧ Let us consider his fullness of grace. The term *grace* suggests two ideas, not far removed from one another: first, of being in favour; second, of being given a present. For we give gratis to those who are after our own heart and to our own liking. We may like them either reservedly or unreservedly; reservedly, when we would give them what is ours, but without entering into intimacy; unreservedly, when we would draw them close to us according to the kind and degree of our liking. Consequently, anybody who has grace has received a gift, but not everybody who has received a gift is held dear. Hence two sorts of grace can be distinguished, one is only a free gift, the other is also a grant of friendship.

Of course by the very force of the idea, grace is never a matter of right.

There are two kinds of right, namely, what is due to what we are and what is due to what we do. The first is involved in the demands of our nature: thus it is due that man should have reason and hands and feet; the second is what we deserve by our acts, for example, the reward for labour. All the gifts freely given to men by God surpass the claims of nature and are not acquired by merit – though supernatural rewards are not without the name and style of grace, for grace is the principle of merit, *the gift of God is eternal life* (Rom. vi. 23), and they are given more abundantly than we deserve.

Now some of these gifts, while exceeding the powers of human nature and granted without our deserving, do not of themselves make us pleasing to God; for example, the gift of prophecy, the working of miracles, special gifts of knowledge and teaching, and so forth. They do not join us to God, though they reflect some divine likeness to God, and have some share in divine goodness, as do all things. But there are also other gifts, freely given, which render us dear to God and united to him.

Union with God can be by affection or by substance. The first is through charity. St. Paul says that without charity all the other gifts *profit us nothing* (1 Cor. xiii. 1–3). Such grace is common to all the saints. The second union is more than an identification by love and divine indwelling, but is the real unity of one single person or hypostasis. Jesus Christ alone has this unity; he is both God and man. This is the singular grace who is joined to God as one single person; a gift freely given, exceeding natural power, rewarding no merits, and making Christ most dear to God: *This is my beloved Son, in whom I am well pleased* (Matt. iii. 17).

Between these graces lies a difference. The first is an habitual state of soul infused by God; the soul cleaves to God by an act of love, a perfect act coming from a habit. But the substantial existence of two natures conjoined in one person is not a habit. The nearer a created reality comes to God the nearer it shares in his goodness and the more lavish the gifts which fill it: the closer the flame the greater the warmth and light. Nothing nearer to God than a human nature hypostatically united to him could exist or be thought of.

As a result Christ's soul is fuller of grace than any other soul. This habitual grace, however, did not lead up to the hypostatic union, but flowed from it. This is suggested by the Evangelist's turn of speech: *We beheld his glory, the glory as of the only begotten of the Father, full of grace and truth* (John i. 14). The man Christ is the only begotten of the Father because he is the Word made flesh, and because he is the Word made flesh was he made full of grace and truth.

The plenitude of nobility is more conspicuous when it gives to others; the brightness of light is judged by the area it illuminates. From Christ's fullness grace is outpoured on us. The Son of God was made man that men might be made gods and become the children of God: *When the fullness of the time was come, God sent forth his Son, made of a woman, made under the law, to redeem them that were under the law, that we might receive the adoption of sons* (Gal. iv. 4–5).

Because of this overflow of grace and truth Christ is called the Head of the Church. Motion and sensation spread from the head to other members within the same organism: *God hath put all things under his feet, and gave him to be the head over all things to the Church, which is his body, the fullness of him that filleth all in all* (Eph. i. 22–23). He can be called the head, not only of men, but also of angels, because of his dignity and efficacy, not because he is himself of angelic nature: *God raised him from the dead, and set him at his own right hand in the heavenly places, far above all principality, and power, and might, and dominion, and every name that is named, not only in this world, but also in that which is to come* (Eph. i. 20–21).

To summarize: theological tradition ascribes to Christ a threefold grace. First, the grace of hypostatic union, whereby a human nature is united in person to the Son of God. Second, sanctifying grace, the fullness of which distinguishes Christ above all others. Third, his grace as head of the Church. All three are duly set out by the Evangelist: first, *the Word was made flesh*; second, *and we beheld his glory, full of grace and truth*; third, *and of his fullness we have all received* (John i. 14, 16).

❦ Next let us consider his fullness of wisdom. At once we reflect that, since in Christ there are two natures, the divine and the human, whatever is credited to either must be doubled. Consequently we profess two wisdoms in Christ, the uncreated wisdom of God and the created wisdom of man. As the Word of God he is the conceived and begotten wisdom of the Father: *Christ the power of God, and the wisdom of God* (1 Cor. i. 24). As a man, two kinds of knowledge can be distinguished, one is godlike, the other springs from human effort.

He beheld God's essence and all things in God: that we are bound to say. For the master-principle of a movement should be high above the process of movement. The vision of God, in which our eternal salvation is achieved, was rightly anticipated in the author of our salvation. We are the subjects of the process; he is the origin. From the beginning of his life he saw God; unlike the blessed he did not arrive at the vision of God.

No one was so near to God. Rightly then was his beatific knowledge greater than any other person's. For there are degrees of vision; God, the cause of all things, is beheld more clearly by some than by others. A cause is seen the more fully the more effects we perceive in it, for the power of a cause is known only by its effects, which, as it were, measure its range. Some gaze on more effects and see their divine meaning better than do others who also see God: theologians work with this clue when they arrange the hierarchies of angels, where the higher ranks instruct the lower. Christ's human soul is set above all other created intelligent substances. With perfect insight he beheld all God's works, past, present, and future. He enlightens the highest angels. In him *are hid all the treasures of wisdom and knowledge* (Col. ii. 3). *All things are naked and opened unto the eyes of him with whom we have to do* (Heb. iv. 13).

Not that his soul attained to comprehension of the Divinity. For comprehending means knowing an object as much as it can be known. God's infinite being is infinite truth, and no created mind, even though knowing the infinite, can know it infinitely, or by seeing God can comprehend him. Christ's soul is created, as all about his human nature was created, otherwise no other nature would exist in Christ apart from the divine nature which alone is uncreated. He is the person of the Word, uncreated and single in two natures: it is for this reason that we do not say that Christ was a creature simply speaking, for his proper name indicates his personality. But we can speak of his body or soul as created. His uncreated wisdom, not his human mind, comprehends God: *No man knoweth the Son but the Father; neither knoweth any man the Father, save the Son* (Matt. xi. 27). His soul, therefore, does not know all God's possible actions, nor all his reasons for acting. All the same, even as man, he is set by God as governor over all creation. Fittingly then he sees in God everything that God does, and in this sense can be called omniscient.

Besides this beatific knowledge in which things are known in the vision of God, there is another mode of knowledge. This starts from creatures themselves. Angels know things in the Word by their morning knowledge; they know things as natural objects in themselves by their evening knowledge. Now this second mode of knowing differs in men and in angels, for men acquire knowledge from their senses, discerning meanings in phenomena through the process of abstraction, whereas angels have an infused knowledge, and carry from their creation the impression of the meaning and likeness of things. Then to both men and angels is given supernatural communication with divine mysteries, and to foster this knowledge angels are enlightened by angels, and men are instructed by prophetic revelation. Since no created nobility should be denied to Christ's soul, which of all souls is the most excellent, it is fitting that, in addition to the beatific vision, three other types of knowledge should also be possessed.

The first is the empirical knowledge which other men also enjoy, for it is proper to human nature that truth should be discovered through the senses. The second is divinely infused, and informs the mind about all truths which human knowledge reaches or can reach, for it is right that the human nature assumed by the Word of God, which restores human nature, should itself lack no human perfection. The third concerns the mystery of grace. Since Christ was not only the restorer of human nature but also the propagator of grace, he also most fully knew those truths exceeding reason which can be perceived by the Gift of Wisdom and the spirit of prophecy.

To sum up: Christ's soul was raised to the highest level of knowledge possible to any created mind, first, as regards seeing God's essence and all things in God, secondly, by knowing the mysteries of grace, and thirdly, all objects of human knowledge. Here no advance was possible. Obviously in course of time Christ's bodily senses grew more experienced about their environment, and therefore his empirical knowledge could increase. *The boy grew in wisdom and stature* (Luke ii. 40). The text can be differently interpreted, to mean, not that he grew wiser, but that his wisdom grew more manifest and instructive to others. It was a providential dispensation to show that he was like other men, for had he displayed adult wisdom in his boyhood, the mystery of the Incarnation might well have appeared a piece of play-acting.

The higher a nature the more intimate what comes from it, for its inwardness of activity corresponds to its rank in being. Inanimate bodies hold the lowest place of all; from them nothing emanates save by the action of one thing on another.

Plants are higher; already in them there is an issuing from within, for the sap is converted into seed, and this when planted in soil grows into a plant. Here the first degree of life may be discerned, for living things are those that set themselves into activity, whereas things that are in motion only inasmuch as they are acted on from outside are lifeless. This is the index of life in plants, that within them there is a principle of motion. Nevertheless, their life is imperfect, for though the emanation is from within at the beginning, that which comes forth gradually becomes wholly extraneous in the end; the blossoms change into fruit distinct from the boughs on which they grow, and presently these, when ripe, fall to the ground and in due course become other plants. Scrutiny shows that the principle of this process is extrinsic to the plant.

Above plants there is a higher grade of life, that namely of sensitive things. Their proper process, though initiated from without, terminates within; the more developed the process, the more intimate this result. A sensible object impresses a form on the external senses, this goes into the imagination and then deeper into the store of memory. What begins from without is thus worked up within, for the sensitive powers are conscious within themselves. So this vital process is superior to that of vegetating proportionately to its greater immanence; but is not yet wholly perfect, since the emanation is always from one thing to another.

The supreme and perfect grade of life is found in mind, which can reflect on itself and understand itself. But there are different degrees of intelligence. The human intellect, though able to know itself, must start from outside objects and cannot know these without sense-images. A more perfect intellectual life is that of pure spirits, where the mind does not proceed by introspection from outside things to know itself, but knows itself by itself. But not yet is the ultimate perfection of life achieved, for though the concept is wholly intrinsic, nevertheless it is not identical with the substance of their mind, since the being and understanding of spiritual creatures are not the same. The highest perfection of life is in God, where understanding is not distinct from being, and where the concept *is* the divine essence.

❧ Concerning the inquiry whether hell is at or near the centre of the earth, my opinion is that nothing should be rashly asserted, not least because Augustine reckoned that nobody knows where hell is. The lower regions can mean whatever is meant by the term *inferior*. For myself I do not believe that man can know the position of hell.

❧ *He watereth the high hills from his chambers; the earth is satisfied with the fruit of thy works* (Ps. ciii. 13 Vulgate).

From eternity the Lord King of Heaven made the law that the gifts of his providence should reach lowly things through intermediate principles, wherefore Dionysius says this to be the holy law of divinity, that they should be led by measured steps to divine light. This law is developed in bodily as well as in spiritual creatures. On this point Augustine remarks, that just as the crasser and weaker bodies are ruled by subtler and more potent bodies according to plan, so are all bodies ruled by the rational spirit of life. And therefore the psalm of our text sings this law, observed in the communication of spiritual truth, through metaphors drawn from things of sense. From the heights of the clouds showers fall and the mountains are watered; thence streams flow down and, drinking them in, the earth is made fruitful. So also from the heights of divine wisdom are watered the minds of teachers, signified by mountains, and through their ministry divine wisdom is shed on the minds of their hearers. Let us consider four points in the text we have cited: the height of spiritual doctrine – the dignity of its teachers – the condition of the hearers – and the method of communication.

(i)

The height is beckoned to by the words, *from his upper rooms*; the Gloss says, *from his higher chambers*. Three comparisons may illustrate how near sacred theology is to the summit of knowledge.

First, by its origin, for this is the wisdom described *as descending from above* (James iii. 17); also, *the word of God on high is the fount of wisdom* (Ecclus. i. 5).

Secondly, because of the rarity of the air. *I dwelt in the highest places* (Ecclus. xxiv. 7). There are some heights of divine wisdom to which all may climb, though with difficulty; as Damascene says, some knowledge of God's being is naturally inborn. *All men see him, everyone beholdeth him afar off* (Job xxxvi. 25). There are other heights to be reached only by the skill of experts, guided by their reason; *that which is known to God is manifest to them* (Rom. i. 19). But the highest peaks are beyond all human reasoning; *hidden from the eyes of all living* (Job xxviii. 21); and again, *he makes his covert in darkness* (Ps. xviii. 11 Vulgate). These are the places where wisdom is said to dwell, and they are discovered to dedicated guides; *thy spirit searcheth all things, yea even the deep things of God* (1 Cor. ii. 10).

Thirdly, because of the sublimity of the end, which is the highest of all, namely eternal life. *These are written that you may believe that Jesus is the Christ, the son of God, and that believing you may have life in his name* (John xx. 31); and again, *seek the things that are above, where Christ is sitting at the right hand of God; mind the things that are above, not the things that are upon the earth* (Col. iii. 1–2).

(ii)

Because this doctrine is awe-inspiring, dignity is demanded of its teachers. They are signified by mountains, *he watereth the high hills*. And this also for three reasons.

First, because of their loftiness, lifted above earth and nigh to heaven.

Theologians should spurn earthly things and gaze with longing at the heights above. *Our conversation is in heaven* (Phil. iii. 20). And it is said of the teacher of teachers, namely Christ; *he shall be exalted above the hills, and all nations shall flow unto him* (Isa. ii. 2).

Secondly, because of their splendour. For hills are the first to reflect the dawn, and similarly holy teachers are the first to catch the light of divine wisdom. *How wonderful was thy dawning over the everlasting hills; dismayed are the rash-hearted* (Ps. lxxv. 5, Vulgate), that is by teachers who are nigh to eternity. *Among whom ye shine as lights in the world* (Phil. ii. 15).

Thirdly, because mountains are a bulwark and protect a country from its enemies. So the teachers in the Church should be defenders of the faith against error. The children of Israel relied, not on lances and arrows, but on their hills; and for this they were sometimes taunted: *You have not gone up to face the enemy, nor have you set a wall for the house of Israel, to stand in battle in the day of the Lord* (Ezek. xiii. 5). Accordingly, all teachers of holy writ should stand out in virtue that they may be fitted to preach, for as Gregory says, it must needs be that the teaching will be contemned of those whose life is despised. *But the words of the wise are goads, and nails deeply fastened in* (Eccles. xii. 11). The pulse cannot beat steadily in the fear of the Lord unless we are trained to heights. Guides must be experienced if they are to be helpful and show us the way. *Unto me, who am less than the least of all the saints, is the grace given, to preach among the gentiles the unsearchable riches of Christ, to make all men see what is the fellowship of the mystery, which hath been hid from the beginning of the world* (Eph. iii. 8–9). So also must they be well equipped to tackle errors. *I will give you mouth and wisdom so that all your adversaries will not be able to gainsay nor resist* (Luke xxi. 15). Concerning these three functions, namely preaching, studying, and disputing, it is said (Tit. i. 9): *that you may be able to exhort*, as regards preaching; *in sound doctrine*, as regards study; and *to convince gainsayers*, as regards disputation.

(iii)

The condition of the hearers is compared to earth, the text saying, *the earth shall be satisfied.* Here again there are three characteristics. The earth is lowest, *the heavens above and the earth beneath* (Prov. xxv. 3). Secondly, it is stable and firm, *the earth standeth for ever* (Eccles. i. 4). Thirdly, it is fruitful, *let the earth bear fresh plants and herbs yielding seeds, and trees bearing fruit after their kind* (Gen. i. 11).

Therefore, like the ground should learners be low according to humility: *where humility is there also is wisdom* (Prov. xi. 2). And firm in soundness of sense: *be no more childish* (Eph. iv. 14). And fruitful, that the words of wisdom may be taken and yield good fruit: *what fell on good ground, these are they who in a good and honest heart hearing the word keep it and bring forth their fruit in patience* (Luke viii. 15). Modesty is required, for they are instructed through listening: *if thou wilt incline thine ear thou shalt receive instruction, and if thou lovest to hear thou shalt be wise* (Ecclus. vi. 33). Also judgement of the right sense of what is meant: *doth not our ear try thy words?* (Job xii. 11). Finally, fruitfulness of discovery, for a good listener takes much from the little he hears: *give occasion to a wise man, and wisdom will be added* (Prov. ix. 9).

(iv)

In conclusion the conditions of communication are touched on and at three points, the method, the quantity, and the quality.

As regards the method of delivery, note that the minds of the teachers cannot grasp the complete plan of divine wisdom. It is not said that the high truths descend into the mountains, but that *he watereth the high hills from his chambers. Lo, these are said in part* (Job xxvi. 14). Similarly, the teacher cannot communicate to his hearers all that he grasps. *He heard unspeakable words which it is not lawful for a man to utter* (2 Cor. xii. 4). The text does not say that the fruit of mountains is given to the earth, but that the earth is satisfied with its own fruits. In expounding the text, *he bindeth up the water in his clouds, so that they break not out and fall down together* (Job xxvi. 8), Gregory says that a teacher should not teach all he knows to unlearned folk, for he himself cannot know of the divine mysteries all they be.

Secondly, the manner of possession is here referred to, for God has wisdom of his nature, and wisdom comes from his own higher parts. *With him is knowledge and strength, he has counsel and understanding* (Job xii. 13). But enough of this knowledge is bestowed on teachers, therefore they are said to be watered from on high. *I will water my garden of plants, with abundance the fruits of my meadow* (Ecclus. xxiv. 35). The hearers share in this, signified by the fruitfulness of earth. *I shall be satisfied when thy glory shall appear* (Ps. xvi. 15, Vulgate).

Thirdly, as regards the authority for teaching. God gives wisdom of his own power, therefore he is said to water the mountains. But human teachers impart wisdom only as ministers. Therefore, the fruits are not attributed to the mountains, but to God's activity: *the earth is satisfied with the fruit of thy works.* For *who then is Paul, and who is Apollos, but ministers by whom ye believed, even as the Lord gave to every man?* (1 Cor. iii. 5).

But who is sufficient for these things? (2 Cor. ii. 16). God demands upright servants; *he that walketh in a perfect way, he shall serve me* (Ps. c. 6). They must be intelligent; *a wise servant is acceptable to the king* (Prov. xiv. 35): and ardent; *who makest thy angels spirits and thy ministers a burning fire* (Ps. ciii. 4): and disciplined; *you ministers of his that do his will* (Ps. cii. 21). Through and of himself no man is equal to such a ministry, but we hope for divine help. *Not that we are sufficient to think anything of ourselves as of ourselves, but our sufficiency is of God* (2 Cor. iii. 5). It should be entreated of him. *If any of you lack wisdom, let him ask of God, that giveth to all liberally and upbraideth not; and it shall be granted him* (James i. 5).

Let us pray that Christ may bestow this wisdom on us: Amen.

❧ The intellective soul confers on the human body all that the sensitive soul confers on animals, and likewise the sensitive soul confers on animals whatever the nutritive principles confer on plants, and more. Any soul in man additional to his intellective soul would therefore be superfluous, for it contains the sensitive soul and with something to spare.

❧ The proposition, *souls are individuated by the matters of bodies, and they keep their individuality when disembodied, as wax the impression of a seal*, can be understood aright though it is also open to misconception. If taken in the sense that bodies are the total cause of the individuation of soul, then the proposition is false; but if the sense is that they are the partial causes, then it is true. The body is not the total cause of the being of soul, though the very being of soul is in relationship to body. Similarly, the body is not the total cause of the individuality of this soul, though it is this soul's nature to be joinable to this body, which relationship remains in the soul after the body's death.

❧ Since all men naturally desire to know the truth, there is a natural desire to avoid error and, given the ability, to confute it. Of all errors the most indecent attack our heritage of mind. One such has sprung from the words of Averroes, who announced that there is a universal and unique mind for all men. We have already argued against this doctrine elsewhere, but our purpose is to write again and at length in refutation, because of the continued impudence of those who gainsay the truth on this head.

Not that we shall be at pains to show that it is contrary to the Christian faith, for this is sufficiently apparent to all. Since mind is the only deathless part of the soul, were the diversity of minds to be fused, the upshot would be that a unique mind alone remained after death, and so there would be no prospect of rewards and punishments. What we intend to do is to show that this error is no less opposed to the principles of philosophy. Because some of the advocates of this doctrine do not hold with the statements of Latin authorities, but base themselves on the positions of the Peripatetics, whose writings, except for those of Aristotle, they have never seen, we shall show that their teaching is clean contrary to his statements. . . .

These,[1] then, are the points we have made to destroy this error, not by the documents of faith, but in the light of Aristotle. If anyone who falsely glories in the name of philosopher still wishes to oppose what we have written, let him not mutter in corners with adolescents who lack discrimination in such arduous questions, but let him come out into the open, and write if he dares. I am the least, but he will find others besides myself who are servants of truth and who will resist his errors and instruct his ignorance.

[1] The argument is summarized in the next extract, where, as in the *de Unitate Intellectus*, St. Thomas writes with unwonted informality and vigour.

❧ That a unique mind should be shared by all men is quite out of the question. If Plato's doctrine be adopted, namely, that man is his mind, then it would follow that, if there were one mind for Socrates and for Plato, there would be one man there, and they would not be distinct from one another except by something outside their essence: the difference between them would be no more than that between the man in a tunic and the same man in a cloak.

The thesis is also impossible on Aristotle's doctrine that the mind is a part or power of the soul, which soul is man's substantial form. For there cannot be a unique form of several things numerically diverse, as it is impossible for them to possess one being.

Indeed, it is an unworkable thesis howsoever the union of mind with this or that man be stated. For obviously, if there be one principal cause and two instruments, you can talk about one agent and many actions; as when a man touches different things with his two hands, there is one toucher, but two touches. Conversely, if there be one instrument and many principal causes, you can talk about one action but many agents; as when a ship is towed by the same cable, despite many towing there is but one pull. If, however, the principal and the instrument are identical, there is then one agent and one action; when the smith smites with one hammer there is one smiter and one smiting. Now it is clear that howsoever and in whatever fashion the mind is united to this or that man, mind is his chief part and the sensitive powers are subservient. If, therefore, you imagined that there were different minds but one sensorium for two men, for instance if two men had one eye in common, there would be one vision, but two people seeing. But if the mind be one, no matter how the other powers used by the mind as instruments were diversified, in no sense could Socrates and Plato be called anything but one intelligence. And if we add that the activity of understanding comes from no other instrument than the power of the mind, it would follow further that there would be one agent and one action – in other words, all men would be one intelligence producing one act of understanding, providing, of course, it was about the same intelligible object.

You might be able to diversify my intellectual action from yours by the diversity of images, namely, because my picture of a stone was different from yours, but only on condition that the image were the form of the vital intellect, which it is not. The mental form is not a sense-image, but a meaning abstracted from it. The same meaning may be abstracted by the same mind from diverse images; a man may have different images of stone and yet abstract from all of them but one meaning. Were there one mind for all men, a diversity of intellectual activity in this man and that man would not be caused just because there were two sets of images. We dismiss this fiction of the great commentator[1] and are left, therefore, with the conclusion that it is quite impossible and highly inconvenient to postulate one mind for all men.

1 Averroes.

❧ While the other virtues perfect a man's own personal state, justice stands out as rendering another man his due. What is correct in their activity is measured by reference to the doer, but what is correct in justice leaves aside this consideration and is measured by what is owing to another. Justice squarely meets this obligation, for instance a fair wage for work done. A deed is termed just when it passes this fundamental test, without reference to the mood in which it is performed, which reference is the test for the other virtues. Rights are the special object of justice.

❧ A right may be another's due on two titles, one from the very nature of things, this is termed natural right; the other from agreement, either private or public, and this is termed positive right.

❧ By common agreement human wills can establish a right in those matters where there is no conflict with natural justice. Wherefore, Aristotle remarks that in their principle legal rights may be such or otherwise, but once they are laid down it is different. What is contrary to natural right cannot be made just by human will. *Woe to those who make iniquitous laws* (Isa. x. 1).

❧ Whether it is lawful for a man to possess a thing as his own? We proceed thus to this article.

It would seem that private property is not lawful. For whatever is contrary to the natural law is unlawful. Now according to the natural law all things are held in common, and the possession of property is contrary to this community of goods. Therefore it is unlawful for any man to appropriate any external thing to himself.

Secondly, the words of the rich man already quoted[1] are expounded by Basil as follows: the rich who reckon that the common goods they have seized are their own properties are like those who go in advance to the theatre excluding others and appropriating to themselves what is intended for common use. Now it would be unlawful to obstruct others from laying their hands on common goods. Therefore it is unlawful to appropriate to oneself what belongs to the community.

Thirdly, Ambrose says, and he is quoted in the Decretals: let no man call his own that which is common. That he is speaking of external things appears from the context. Therefore it seems unlawful for a man to appropriate an external thing to himself.

But on the contrary Augustine writes of the Apostolics, or those who gave themselves that name with extreme arrogance, who did not admit into communion persons who use marriage or possess property of their own, people such as monks and many clerics in the Catholic Church. The reason why these Apostolics were heretics was that they separated themselves from the Church by allowing no hope of salvation to those who enjoyed the use of these things which they themselves went without. Therefore it is erroneous to maintain that it is unlawful for a man to possess property.

In explanation let me declare that two elements enter into human competence in appropriating external things, the administration and the enjoyment. The first is the power to take care of them and manage them, and here it is lawful for one man to possess property: indeed it is necessary for human living and on three grounds. First, because each man is more careful in looking after what is in his own charge than what is common to many or to all; in the latter case each would shirk the work and leave to another that which concerns the community, as we see

[1] In a passage not printed here, the author quotes from a parable (Luke xii. 18) in which a rich man exclaims, *I will pull down my barns and build greater, and there will I bestow all my fruits and my goods.*

when there is a great number of servants. Secondly, because human affairs are conducted in a more orderly fashion when each man is charged with taking care of some particular thing himself, whereas there would be confusion if anyone took charge of anything indeterminately. Thirdly, because a more peaceful state is preserved when each man is contented with what is his own. Hence we observe that quarrels arise more frequently among people who share in common and without division of goods.

The second element in human competence concerns the enjoyment of material things. Here man ought to possess them, not as his own, but as common, to the extent of being ready to communicate them to others in their need. Hence St. Paul says: *Charge the rich of this world to give easily, to communicate to others*, &c. (1 Tim. vi. 17–18).

In reply to the first objection, it should be said that community of goods is attributed to the natural law, not in the sense that natural law dictates that all possessions should be in common and that nothing should be possessed as one's own, but in the sense that the division of possessions is not made by natural law but by human agreement, which belongs to positive law. Hence private ownership is not contrary to natural law, but is an addition to it devised by human reason.

To the second objection: a man would not act unfairly if he went beforehand to the theatre in order to prepare the way for others; what is unfair is blocking the enjoyment of others from going. Similarly, a rich man does not act unlawfully if he encloses what was common at the beginning and gives others a share. But he sins if he indiscriminately excludes others from the benefit. Hence Basil says, How can you abound in wealth while another begs, unless it be that you may obtain the merit of good stewardship and he be crowned with the rewards of patience?

To the third objection: Ambrose is referring to ownership as regards enjoyment, wherefore he adds that he who spends too much is a robber.

❦ There are three conditions of a just war. First, the authority of the sovereign by whose command the war is to be waged. For it is not the business of the private individual to declare war or to summon the nation. The second condition is that hostilities should begin because of some crime on the part of the enemy. Wherefore Augustine observes that a just war is wont to be described as one that avenges wrongs, when a nation or state has to be punished for refusing to make amends for the injuries done by its people or to restore what has been seized unjustly. The third condition is a rightful intention, the advancement of good or the avoidance of evil. It may happen that a war declared by legitimate authority for a just cause may yet be rendered unlawful through a wicked intention. Hence Augustine declares that the passion of inflicting harm, the cruel thirst for vengeance, a plundering and implacable spirit, the fever of turmoil, the lust of power and suchlike, all these are justly condemned in war.

☙ Always remember that political science is supreme, not unconditionally, but in relation to the other practical sciences which deal with human matters and whose purposes are social. For theology, which considers the final end of the entire universe, is of all sciences the most important.

☙ Man is a social animal, having many wants he cannot supply for himself. He is born into a group by nature. By living with others he is helped to the good life. And this on two heads.

First, as regards necessities without which life cannot be lived, he is supported by the domestic group. He depends on his parents for his birth, feeding, upbringing. Each member of the family helps the others.

Secondly, as regards the conveniences without which life cannot be lived well, he is helped by the civil group, both for material benefit, for the State provides public services beyond the means of one household, and for moral advantage, thus public authority can check young criminals when paternal warnings go unheeded.

Bear in mind that family and civil groups are unities, not because they are single organisms, but because they are composed of different substances arranged in order; consequently there is a proper activity for a part of such a whole, and this is not a group-activity; a soldier may have interests that are no part of army life and discipline. Conversely the group as a whole manifests operations which are not proper to any of its members, for instance the tactical conduct of an army in battle or the general handling of a ship.

For there are other wholes which are closer unities. The parts are continuous, compacted together, or combining to constitute one nature, and the result is one thing simply speaking, or one substance. In such cases no part is active without the whole being engaged. Movements of parts and of wholes involve one another, and consequently they should be discussed by one and the same science.

In treating of artificial wholes the same department of science does not deal with the whole as well as with the parts. On this account moral science is divided into three sections: the first is individual and takes the activity of one man as directed to his own personal end; the second, termed economic, takes the functional purpose of the family; and the third, termed political, takes the operations of the civilian group.

To be a social and political animal[1] living in a crowd is even more natural to man than to the other animals. His inherited needs declare this dependence. Nature provides food for other animals, covering, weapons of defence, teeth and claws, or at least swiftness of flight. But with man it is different; instead he is endowed with his reason by which he can contrive these aids. Yet to see to all of them is beyond any one man's power; alone he cannot dispatch the business of living. Consequently that he should dwell in association with many is according to his nature.

Furthermore, other animals havc an inborn ingcnuity with rcgard to what is beneficial or harmful; a sheep instinctively recognizes that a wolf is a menace, and other animals similarly take advantage of medicinal herbs and other things needful to life. But man's inbred knowledge about these matters is limited to general principles; he has to take pains to work from them to the provision of his needs in each and every case. One solitary man cannot discover everything for himself. He must combine in a team, so that one may help another and different men be reasonably engaged in different jobs, one in medicine, another in this, another in that.

This is made plain by the fact that it is peculiar to man to use language, through which he can adequately disclose his thoughts to another. Other

[1] Note the addition of *social* to Aristotle's *political.*

animals may express their common emotions to one another, a dog by barking and other animals by appropriate signs. But man is more communicative, even more so than the gregarious animals, such as storks, ants, and bees. With this in mind, Solomon says: *It is better that two should be together than solitary; for they gain by their mutual companionship* (Eccles. iv. 9).

☙ The greater the friendship the more permanent it should be. The greatest friendship is that between man and wife; they are coupled not only by physical intercourse, which even among animals conduces to a certain sweet friendship, but also for the sharing of domestic life. In sign whereof is it declared: *a man should leave father and mother for the sake of his wife* (Gen. ii. 24).

☙ Marriage is called true when it achieves its proper perfection. The perfection of anything is twofold, primary and secondary. The first consists in a thing's form, which constitutes it as a thing of a definite kind. The second consists in the activity through which in some manner it reaches its end. The form of marriage lies in an inseparable union of minds by which either is unalterably plighted to serve the other loyally. The end of marriage is the begetting and rearing of children.

☙ Promiscuity is contrary to human nature. Intimacy should be reserved to one man with one particular woman, with whom he remains, not briefly, but for a long period, or even for good: this is called matrimony.

☙ Two points should be observed concerning the healthy constitution of a state or nation. One is that all should play a responsible part in the governing: this ensures peace, and the arrangement is liked and maintained by all. The other concerns the type of government; on this head the best arrangement for a state or government is for one to be placed in command, presiding by authority over all, while under him are others with administrative powers, yet for the rulers to belong to all because they are elected by and from all. Such is the best policy, well combined from the different strains of monarchy, since there is one at the head; of aristocracy, since many are given responsibility; and of democracy, since the rulers are chosen from and by the people.

❧ If by nature men are to live together, then the group they form must needs be ruled. With many individuals each seeking what suits himself, the mass would disintegrate were there not one power within it caring for the common good. Any organism would disintegrate were there no unifying force working for the common good of all the members. Solomon says, *Where there is no governor, the people shall be scattered* (Prov. xi. 14), and with good warrant, for private and common pull different ways. People fall apart by their private interests and come together by their common interests. Of diverse things there are diverse causes. A ruling cause therefore is required, standing apart from interests of private gain, to act for the common good of the many.

The purpose proper to a group of freemen is different from that of a group of slaves, for a freeman is his own master while a slave belongs to another. Therefore, if a group of freemen be directed by the ruler to the common good, the government will be fair and right, worthy of freemen. But if the aim be not the common good, but the private benefit of the ruler, then the government will be unfair and crooked.[1] *Woe to shepherds who feed themselves*, that is, those who seek their own advantage. *Should not the sheep be fed by the shepherd?* (Ezek. xxxiv. 2).

There are three types of deviation from fair government, corresponding to the ruling class that is out to secure its own private interests. If the government is run by one man then he is called a tyrant, a word having the sense of unregulated mastery in its derivation, for a tyrant bears down by sheer force and does not guide in accordance with law; hence in antiquity a man of might was called a tyrant. If it is in the hands of a few then the régime is called an oligarchy, when several men, taking advantage of their wealth, oppress the people like a tyrant multiplied. If power is wielded by the common masses at the expense of men of property then the régime is called a democracy, when the majority amounts to a tyrant writ large.

A fair constitution is similarly graded. When the administration is conducted by the whole community, and chiefly by those ready to

[1] The argument turns on the difference between a slave, who is a utility, and a freeman, who is not a means to anyone's advantage.

defend the commonwealth, the régime is called by the general name of polity. If the administration is in the hands of a few but right-minded magnates, the régime is called an aristocracy, the rule of the best, and these therefore receive the title of nobles. If the government is one man's responsibility, then he is properly named king. *And David my servant shall be king over them; and they shall have one shepherd* (Ezek. xxxvii. 24). Hence it is essential to kingship that one man should be sovereign and that he should be a good shepherd, seeking the common good of the people and not his own private profit.[1]

❧ Lordship may be taken in two senses: either as the opposite of slavery – and then a lord means somebody to whom another is subject as a slave; or by and large with reference to subjects of any kind – and then any man who has the office of ruling and directing freemen may be called a lord. In the state of innocence one man could have been another's master in the latter sense, but not in the former.

The root of the matter is that a slave differs from a freeman because, as Aristotle says, a freeman exists for himself, whereas a slave exists for another's sake. A slave-owner is one who disposes of other people for his own advantage entirely. Since each man desires his own proper benefit and feels it a grievous situation to abandon to another what belongs to himself, such domination inevitably implies hardship for the subject, and therefore would not have been present between man and man had there been no lapse into sin.

But a freeman may have a ruler over him when he is directed for his own good or for the common good. Such dominion would have existed apart from sin, and for two reasons. First, because man is instinctively a social animal, and even in a state of innocence men would have lived

[1] These three classical types of political constitution, together with their three caricatures, are not dwelt on by St. Thomas. So long as the government is set on the common good, which of the three tolerable types is emphasized will depend on historical circumstances. He himself prefers a constitution well blent of all three. Elsewhere he notes that the mere numbers of the governing class do not settle the type of constitution. An aristocracy is not necessarily an oligarchy, still less a plutocracy; a democracy not necessarily the majority rule of a working class unable to enjoy leisure, still less the rule of the mob. Though he approves of *status popularis*, the word *democracy* still keeps the ugly sense it had for Plato. *Populus*, it should be noted, is not *plebs*, but includes all citizens of the commonwealth.

sociably together. When many people are involved, one man should preside to watch over the common good, for many as such exert themselves for different things, whereas one keeps a single end in view. Hence Aristotle says that when many work with a common purpose we always find a unified command at the head. Secondly, pre-eminent gifts of intelligence and character would be embarrassing unless they were serviceable for others, according to St. Peter, *as every man hath received grace, ministering the same one to another* (1 Pet. iv. 10). And St. Augustine speaks about the commanders, who are indeed the servants of those they seem to command, ruling not in ambition, but as bound by careful duty; not in domineering, but in nourishing pity. Thus hath nature's order prescribed, and man by God was thus created.

❦ Obedience is commanded within the limits of due observance. The duty develops according to the gradation of authorities which have power, not only over temporalities, but also spiritually over the conscience. St. Paul says, *let every soul be subject unto the higher powers, for there is no power but of God* (Rom. xiii. 1). Therefore a Christian should obey power that is from God, but not otherwise.

Power may not stem from God for two reasons: it may be defective either in its origins or in its exercise.

Concerning the first, the defect may lie either in the personal unworthiness of the man or in some flaw in the manner of obtaining high position – violence, bribery, or some other illicit practice. The former is no bar to the possession of legitimate authority; and because the very form of office is from God, who also causes the duty of obedience, it follows that subjects are bound to obey such a ruler, though as a man he is a good-for-nothing. The latter, however, is a bar, for a man who has snatched power by violence is no true superior or lord, and whoever has the ability may rightly reject him, unless perhaps the power has been subsequently legitimized by the consent of subjects or by higher authority.

The abuse of power may take two directions. Either the ruler imposes what is contrary to the purpose for which authority is instituted, for instance if he dictates vices contrary to the virtues authority is supposed to promote and sustain. In that event, not merely is a man not bound to obey, he is also bound not to obey, following the martyrs, who suffered death rather than carry out the wicked decrees of tyrants. Or the ruler may make demands where his warrant does not run, for instance in exacting tributes to which he has no title, or something of the sort. In such cases a subject is not bound to obey, neither is he bound not to obey.[1]

❧ There can be two conditions of peoples. One is that of a free people, able to frame laws for itself. Here the consent of the people to an observance, manifested by custom, is of greater force than the authority of the prince, who does not possess the power of framing laws except in so far as he is the public authority representing the people, for though no particular person can enact laws the whole people can. The other condition is that of a people who do not enjoy the unfettered power of making their own laws or of abrogating the laws of a higher ruler. Nevertheless, even here prevailing custom obtains the force of law so long as it is permitted, and therefore approved, by those whose business it is to legislate.

❧ By nature all men are equal in liberty, but not in other endowments. One man is not subordinate to another as though he were a utility. Therefore, in a state of integrity there would have been no overlordship of domination such as would have abolished the liberty of subjects, but only an authority of administration without prejudice to liberty.

❧ Laws are passed to ensure the smooth running of the commonwealth. Unrestricted rights are not allowed in any civil constitution. Even in a democratic state, where the whole people exercise power, rights are not absolute but relative, though from the equal liberty of all subjects under the law the state may be described as predominantly egalitarian. The

[1] St. Thomas has little to say on the legal title to sovereignty. It may be noted however that his sympathies did not seem to lie with those lawyers who held that the people had irrevocably transferred their powers to the prince. He gives no support to the doctrine of the Divine Right of Kings. He is clearly opposed to political absolutism. Yet his ideal of the constitutional and representative monarch, together with his respect for order and well-distributed responsibility and property, may be read, too easily for the historian, in terms of democratic liberalism.

statutes passed by a democracy may be just, not because they reach pure and perfect justice, but because they fit the purpose of the régime.

❧ The disregard of the common good is greater under an oligarchy than under a democracy, where, after all, the welfare of the majority has been attempted. But sorriest of all is a tyranny where the advantage of one man is sought. As the rule of a king is best, so the rule of a tyrant is worst.

Security is banished and everything is uncertain when people are cut off from law and depend on the will, I would even say the greed, of another. A tyrant oppresses the bodies of his subjects, but, what is more damnable, he threatens their spiritual growth, for he is set on his own power, not their progress. He is suspicious of any dignity they may possess that will prejudice his own iniquitous domination. A tyrant is more fearful of good men than of bad men, for he dreads their strange virtue.

Fearful lest they grow strong and so stout of heart as no longer to brook his wicked despotism, but resolve in companionship to enjoy the fruits of peace, a tyrant is constrained to destroy good men's confidence in one another, lest they band together to throw off his yoke. Therefore he sows discord among them, and encourages dissensions and litigation. He forbids celebrations that make for good fellowship, weddings and feastings and suchlike that are wont to promote familiarity and mutual loyalty.

When they are brought up under such a régime of fear men inevitably degenerate. They become mean-spirited and averse from many and strenuous feats.

IHS

Lauda, Sion, Salvatórem,
lauda ducem et pastórem
in hymnis et cánticis.

Quantem potes, tantum aude:
quia major omni laude,
nec laudáre súfficis.

Laudis thema speciális,
panis vivus et vitális
hódie propónitur.

Quem in sacrae mensa coenae
turbae fratrum duodénae
datum non ambígitur.

Sit laus plena, sit sonóra,
sit jucunda, sit decóra
mentis jubilátio.

Dies enim sollemnis ágitur
in qua mensae prima recólitur
hujus institútio.

Sion, to your Saviour sing,
to your Shepherd and your King,
let the air with praises ring!

All you can proclaim with mirth,
for far higher is His worth
than the glory words may wing.

Lo! before our eyes and living
is the sacred bread life-giving,
theme of canticle and hymn.

We profess this bread from Heaven
to the Twelve by Christ was given,
for our faith rests firm in Him.

Let us form a joyful chorus,
may our lauds ascend sonorous
bursting from each loving breast,

For we solemnly record
how the Table of the Lord
with the Lamb's own gift was blest.

In hac mensa novi Regis
novum Pascha novae legis
Phase vetus términat.

On this altar of the King
this new Paschal Offering
brings an end to ancient rite.

Vetustátem nóvitas
umbram fugit véritas
noctem lux elíminat.

Shadows flee that truth may stay,
oldness to the new gives way
and night's darkness to the light.

Quod in coena Christus gessit,
faciéndum hoc expréssit
in sui memóriam.

What at supper Christ completed
he ordained to be repeated
in His memory divine.

Docti sacris institútis,
panem, vinum in salútis
consecrámus hóstiam.

Wherefore now, with adoration,
we the Host of our salvation
consecrate from bread and wine.

Dogma datur Christiánis,
quod in carnem transit panis
et vinum in sánguinem.

Words do nature's course derange
that in Flesh the bread may change
and the wine in Christ's own blood.

Quod non capis, quod non vides,
animósa firmat fides,
praeter rerum órdinem.

Does it pass your comprehending?
Faith the law of light transcending
leaps to things not understood.

Sub divérsis speciébus,
signis tantum, et non rebus,
latent res exímiae.

Here beneath these signs are hidden
priceless things to sense forbidden;
signs, not things, are all we see.

Caro cibus sanguis potus:
manet tamen Christus totus
sub utráque spécie.

Flesh from bread, and Blood from wine:
yet is Christ in either sign
all entire confessed to be.

A suménte non concísus,
non confráctus, non divísus:
integer accípitur.

And all who of Him do partake
sever not, nor rend, nor break:
all entire their Lord receive.

Sumit unus, sumunt mille:
quantum isti, tantum ille:
nec sumptus consúmitur.

Whether one or thousand eat,
all receive the selfsame meat,
nor do less for others leave.

Sumunt boni, sumunt mali:
sorte tamen inaequáli
vitae vel intéritus.

Both the wicked and the good
eat of this celestial Food –
but with ends how opposite!

Mors est malis, vita bonis:
vide, paris sumptiónis
quam sit dispar éxitus,

With this most substantial Bread
unto life or death they're fed,
with a difference infinite –

Fracto demum sacraménto,
ne vacíllis, sed meménto,
tantum esse sub fragménto,
quantum toto tégitur.

Nor a single doubt retain
when they break the Host in twain
but that in every part remain
what was in the whole before.

Nulla rei fit scissúra:
signi tantum fit fractúra:
qua nec status ncc statúra
signatí minúitur.

For the outward sign alone
may some change have undergone,
while the Signified stays one
and the same forevermore.

Ecce panis Angelórum,
factus cibus viatórum:
vere panis filiórum,
non mitténdus cánibus.

Hail, Bread of Angels! broken
for us pilgrims food, and token
of the promise by Christ spoken
His own's meat, not those outside.

In figúris praesignátur,
cum Isaac immolátur:
agnus paschae deputátur:
datur manna pátribus.

Show in Isaac's dedication,
in the Manna's preparation,
in the Paschal immolation,
in old types pre-signified.

Bone pastor, panis vere,
Jesu, nostri miserére:
tu nos pasce, nos tuére:

Jesus, Pastor, bread so pure,
support the weak and shield the poor.
Pity all who pardon seek,

tu nos bona fac vidére
in terra vivéntium.

Tu, qui cuncta scis et vales:
qui nos pascis hic mortales:
tuos ibi commensáles,
coherédis et sodáles
fac sanctórum civium.

Amen. Alleluja.

those who place all trust in You,
hopeful of eternity.

Source of all we have or know,
feed and lead us here below.
Grant that with Your saints above
sitting at the feast of love
we may see You face to face.

Amen. Alleluja.

The English version of the *Corpus Christi* sequence has been adapted by the editor from that in *St. Andrew Daily Missal*, by Dom Gaspar Lefebvre, O.S.B. (E. M. Lohmann Co., St. Paul, Minn.)